Your $\mathcal{M}ALTESE$

By Dr. Robert J. Berndt

Compiled and Edited by
William W. Denlinger and R. Annabel Rathman

DENLINGER'S
Box 76, Fairfax, Virginia 22030

Pictured on the front cover of this book is Ch. Spring Holly Passin' Fancy. On the back cover is Ch. Cotterell's Rascals Tid Bit and two of his sons.

Pictured on the page facing this one is the Author, Dr. Robert J. Berndt, and Manny.

Foreword

Your Maltese is designed as a manual for the pet owner as well as the exhibitor of show Maltese. The advice offered here is of a practical nature and is the result of years of first-hand experience the Author has gained through breeding and showing Maltese. It is hoped that this book will save other dog owners from some of the difficulties encountered by the Author while he was learning about the breed.

It truly would be impossible to express gratitude to each individual who made a contribution to this book. Recognition should, however, be given to all those who furnished photographs. Their sharing of these pictures has made it possible to present a panorama of winning Maltese from all parts of the country.

I do wish to offer a special note of appreciation to Mr. and Mrs. Robert Craig of Good Time Kennel, who introduced me to the Maltese. Their guidance and friendship through the years have been valued highly.

Special thanks also go to Dr. Vicenzo Calvaresi of Villa Malta Kennel for the discussions we have had about the Maltese and for his kindness to me while I was visiting his kennel; to Mrs. J. P. Antonelli of Aennchen Kennel for her constant willingness to help the novice and for her enthusiasm for the breed; to Mrs. Peggy A. Hogg of Morgantown Kennel for having taught me how to groom dogs; to Mr. Maxwell Riddle for the photograph of the Brazilian champion he brought back from a judging assignment in Brazil; and to Dr. Bernice Warren for her help in editing the manuscript of this book as well as that of my earlier book, *Your Lhasa Apso*.

R. J. B.

Contents

Ch. Cotterell's Rascals Tid Bit and one of his sons. Bred and owned by Agnes Cotterell.

The Maltese Puppy

The energetic little white Maltese is a bundle of fluff that seems to shout out to the world, "love me!" And the truth of the matter is that almost everyone does fall in love with this diminutive clown. The Maltese has long been one of the most favored dogs in show ring competition and frequently brings bursts of spontaneous applause from the spectators. Some Maltese have gone all the way to the top in competition simply because of the urgings of the crowd.

A Maltese makes an ideal house pet because of his modest demands for physical space. He does not need the huge exercise yards that larger dogs require, nor is he a disrupting influence in the house because of his size. His boundless energy and his joy in living make him an ideal companion. For his size, he has strength in excess. He can easily leap up on a bed, which is equivalent to a German Shepherd's leaping up to the roof of a single story house. He is a substantial and very sound little dog.

Purchasing a family pet is an exciting event but not one that takes place every day. Since it is such an important happening, careful planning should precede the actual purchase of the puppy. The family should take several trips to well-established breeding kennels and should attend at least one dog show to see examples of the breed at various stages of development from puppyhood to full adulthood.

Once these preliminary steps have been taken, and the family decides to buy a Maltese, then a reputable kennel should be selected for the purchase. If there is a local kennel club and it has a kennel referral service, the problem is simplified. However, since many towns do not have such a service available, it might be necessary to consult one of the national dog magazines. These magazines usually contain classified advertisements arranged in a geographical index which will simplify finding a kennel within easy driving distance. There are a number of breeders located across the country who are dedicated to the betterment of the breed and who will make a great effort in helping the prospective buyer find just the right puppy.

It may be possible to find a half-grown dog that is less expensive than a puppy. A six-month-old dog may not, however, be a good buy, for it is sometimes more difficult for the older dog to make the necessary adjustment as a family pet. A great deal will depend on the personality of the individual dog.

In larger cities the classified section of the newspaper will have a column advertising pets for sale. This is also a valuable source of information for finding a kennel. Commercial pet shops located in shopping centers frequently have a large selection of various breeds readily available. Most pet shops will sell pets on time payments, which makes them especially attractive to some prospective buyers.

Most pet shop owners do not breed their own dogs and so in turn must find breeders who will supply them with their stock. By dealing directly with a breeder, therefore, one can save time, and possibly a little money.

The selection of the individual puppy may depend on a number of factors. Both male and female Maltese make good pets. Both can be housebroken by the usual methods. Males are usually less expensive because they are more numerous than females. This over-supply will keep the price of the males lower. A lower price for males, however, would not necessarily be the case for a show-quality dog.

A puppy should not be taken from his dam before he is eight weeks old. He may be weaned by the time he is six weeks of age, but the extra two weeks will give the puppy greater stamina and more confidence when he finally does leave home. The puppy also has additional time to adjust to a solid food diet, and the breeder has time to have the puppies checked for worms and to have them inoculated.

When there are several puppies to choose from, one has an opportunity to see the personality of each puppy as it relates to the rest of the litter. Whether one is intrigued by the most aggressive and outgoing or develops a protective attitude toward the most shy and retiring, a prospective buyer does get a clue to the future personality of the dog by observing this puppy-play. Maturity and a new home environment can certainly modify a personality, but usually some of the original traits will remain.

While watching the puppy romp, the prospective buyer is able to make certain the puppy does not limp or have any other obvious physical disability. The buyer should examine the puppy to ascertain that his eyes are clear and that he has no sores or cuts on his body. Once this superficial physical examination has been completed, the buyer has an opportunity to make such other rather subjective decisions as those relating to size and overall balance. In many cases, however, a prospective buyer falls in love with a particular puppy and decides to buy that one regardless of other factors to be considered or any predetermined requirements that he might have established. Many dogs are sold to compulsive buyers.

The following weight chart shows a typical growth pattern for a litter of Maltese puppies from whelping to nine weeks of age:

	Mike	Mary	May
at whelping	5.0 oz.	5.0 oz.	5.5 oz.
first week	8.5	8.5	9.5
second week	14.5	13.5	15.5
third week	1# 3.0	1# 1.5	1# 3.5
fourth week	1# 7.5	1# 5.0	1# 7.5
fifth week	1# 11.0	1# 8.0	1# 10.0
sixth week	1# 15.0	1# 11.5	1# 12.0
seventh week	2# 2.0	1# 14.5	1# 15.0
eighth week	2# 4.5	2# 1.5	2# 2.5
ninth week	2# 7.0	2# 4.0	2# 5.0
at maturity	5# 8.0	5# 2.0	5# 4.0

This weight chart can serve as a guide to the future size of a Maltese puppy. A dog maturing at five pounds will weigh about two pounds at two months of age. A variation in this puppy weight will be reflected proportionately in the dog's mature weight.

The quantity and texture of hair of the Maltese should be studied. A puppy that has a very sparse and short coat will probably never have a very heavy one. On the other hand, a puppy with great quantities of dense, soft hair will probably always have a good coat, but this fast growing coat will require a lot of brushing to keep it free from mats and tangles. Since many pet owners do not intend to keep up a full coat, quantity and texture may not be important considerations in the selection of a puppy. An adult dog can always be kept clean and neat by trimming the coat. The dog will lose the typical Maltese look when he is trimmed, but if the owner does not have the necessary time to keep the full adult coat brushed properly, the dog will be much more comfortable than if he is left ungroomed.

9

Before leaving on the final trip to purchase a puppy, one should make sufficient preparations for bringing the puppy home. The easiest way to bring the puppy home is to use a cardboard box that has a lid which can be closed if the puppy gets nervous and tries to jump out. Several layers of folded newspapers should be placed in the bottom of the box and should be covered by a layer of shredded newspapers or an old towel to help absorb any accidents that might occur.

The puppy will usually sit quietly in the box if he is talked to and if someone will pet him and calm him during the drive home. Occasionally a puppy will become excessively excited and try to climb out of the box. If a firm, calming hand is not enough to keep the puppy confined, closing the lid and talking to him will at least keep the puppy where he should be during the drive. Later on, short drives in the car will accustom the puppy to riding and will make trips to the veterinarian or long drives on vacation much more pleasant for both dog and owner.

As soon as the new puppy arrives home, he should be allowed to romp in a fenced exercise area in the yard. This will establish, from the very first moment the puppy is in his new home, that he is to do certain things outside. Returning the puppy to this same place frequently and on a fixed schedule will start the housebreaking pattern promptly and should prove to be a most effective method.

Within a day or two after the purchase, the puppy should be taken to the veterinarian. The puppy undoubtedly will have been given a temporary inoculation by the kennel owner from whom he was purchased, but this temporary shot will be good only for a period of about two weeks. A permanent inoculation can be given when the puppy is three months old. This precaution is extremely important for the health of the puppy and should never be neglected.

There are three common diseases to which dogs are susceptible. They are distemper, hepatitis, and leptospirosis. These diseases are to be considered serious because they are frequently fatal when immunization has been neglected. Even though they are serious diseases, there are effective inoculations against all three. A three-in-one shot can be administered by the veterinarian, followed at a later date by a booster shot. When the puppy is six months old, he should also receive immunization against rabies.

While the puppy is at the veterinarian's, his nails should be clipped. Long nails cause discomfort to the dog when he walks.

Celia's Debonaire Manikin, owned by Priscilla A. Brown and Mrs. Paul S. Wilson, winning the Specialty Sweepstakes.

Ch. Alpond's Sky Rockette, owned by Mrs. Frances C. Geraghty, finishing at the Specialty from the Puppy Class.

Ch. Limerick Popinjay's Pride, owned by Jacky Seger, went Winners Dog from the Puppy Class at the 1972 Maltese Specialty.

Ch. Aennchen's Poona Dancer, owned by F. E. Oberstar and L. G. Ward.

Ch. Aennchen's Sitar Dancer, owned by Mrs. J. P. Antonelli.

Ch. Good Time Chatterbox Lynn with the Author.

Am. & Can. Ch. Nyssamead's Disa, owned by Sharmion Aune.

The owner should learn to clip the dog's nails, for they must be clipped every ten days. Learning to perform this simple chore can save a great deal of money for the owner over a period of time. (For more information on this procedure, see page 38.) Also, while the dog is at the veterinarian's, his ears should be checked to see that they are free from hair and wax. The dog should also be checked to make certain that he is free from worms and other parasites.

A competent veterinarian will keep the dog in good health and help to assure a life of ten to twelve years for the Maltese as well as to keep the owner from needless care and worry. The selection of the right veterinarian is a matter that should warrant serious consideration.

When the new owner purchases the puppy, he will receive from the breeder a blue registration certificate issued by The American Kennel Club, and a copy of the pedigree. The registration certificate will contain the necessary information for completing the transfer of ownership from the breeder to the new owner. The paper contains such information as the names of the sire and the dam, the date of whelping, the color and sex of the puppy, and the registration number of the litter.

At the time of purchase, the breeder must fill in certain information on the reverse side of the registration certificate. This will transfer ownership of the puppy to the new owner. The certificate must be signed by the owner and forwarded to The American Kennel Club along with the fee specified on the certificate.

When filling in the information on the front of the certificate, the owner will also have an opportunity to name the puppy. Two names must be submitted. The first choice will be accepted unless it has already been used for another dog.

When the certificate is returned by The American Kennel Club, it should be kept in a safe place, for it represents the title of ownership of the dog. Information contained in this document will be needed should the dog ever be entered in competition at a sanctioned show, or should the dog be used for breeding.

Ch. Bobbelee Hanky Panky, owned by Mrs. Roberta Harrison.

Ch. Duncan's Nicholas, owned by Muriel K. Calhoun.

Ch. Golden Glow Buz Buz, owned by Mrs. Elva U. McGilbry.

Ch. Joanne-Chen's Indi Dancer, owned by Mr. & Mrs. James Clifton.

The Adult Maltese

The American Kennel Club (A.K.C.) recognizes only purebred dogs. It establishes rules for the breeding of these dogs and offers guidance to the breeders.

The first step that must be taken in gaining A.K.C. recognition is to establish a Standard for the breed. This Standard is a detailed description for the particular breed and can be used as a measuring device for evaluating dogs of that breed. The Standard is the result of the efforts of the breeders who have sought A.K.C. recognition. Over a period of years they must have maintained careful breeding records and must have acted as a semiofficial registering agency for all information. This includes litter registrations, studbooks, and other information pertinent to the development of the breed—such as history and evolution, and records of dogs imported and exported.

After a probationary period in which the consistency of the breed has been demonstrated, The American Kennel Club will allow the breed to be exhibited in the Miscellaneous Class at dog shows. Following a period of time during which the judges have had an opportunity to become familiar with the breed, and the exhibitors have had an opportunity to demonstrate that there is sufficient interest, the breed will be officially recognized and shown in regular breed and Group competition.

At the time of recognition, the Standard of the breed is formally accepted by the A.K.C. Judges and breeders use this official description in determining the quality of the dogs. Standards are, however, difficult to prepare and to interpret. Size and weight descriptions present no problems, but when adjectives appear in abundance, it is difficult to interpret the exact meaning of the writers. Because tastes cahnge from time to time and new breeders become dominant in the breed clubs, Standards may be rewritten. Such evolutionary changes help to explain why pictures of breed winners of twenty or thirty years ago appear quite different from those of dogs winning today.

The following is the official Standard for the Maltese, adopted by The American Kennel Club on November 12, 1963.

STANDARD OF THE MALTESE

General Appearance—The Maltese is a toy dog covered from head to foot with a mantle of long, silky, white hair. He is gentle-mannered and affectionate, eager and sprightly in action, and despite his size, possessed of the vigor needed for the satisfactory companion.

Head—Of medium length and in proportion to the size of the dog. The skull is slightly rounded on top, the stop moderate. The drop ears are rather low set and heavily feathered with long hair that hangs close to the head. Eyes are set not too far apart; they are very dark and round, their black rims enhancing the gentle yet alert expression. The muzzle is of medium length, fine and tapered but not snipy. The nose is black. The teeth meet in an even, edge-to-edge bite, or in a scissors bite.

Neck—Sufficient length of neck is desirable as promoting a high carriage of the head.

Body—Compact, the height from the withers to the ground equaling the length from the withers to the root of the tail. Shoulder blades are sloping, the elbows well knit and held close to the body. The back is level in topline, the ribs well sprung. The chest is fairly deep, the loins taut, strong and just slightly tucked up underneath.

Tail—A long-haired plume carried gracefully over the back, its tip lying to the side over the quarter.

Legs and Feet—Legs are fine-boned and nicely feathered. Forelegs are straight, their pastern joints well knit and devoid of appreciable bend. Hind legs are strong and moderately angulated at stifles and hocks. The feet are small and round, with toe pads black. Scraggly hairs on the feet may be trimmed to give a neater appearance.

Coat and Color—The coat is single, that is, without undercoat. It hangs long, flat, and silky over the sides of the body almost, if not quite, to the ground. The long head-hair may be tied up in a topknot or it may be left hanging. Any suggestion of kinkiness, curliness, or woolly texture is objectionable. Color, pure white. Light tan or lemon on ears is permissible, but not desirable.

Size—Weight under 7 pounds, with from 4 to 6 pounds preferred. Over-all quality is to be favored over size.

Gait—The Maltese moves with a jaunty, smooth, flowing gait. Viewed from the side, he gives an impression of rapid movement, size considered. In the stride, the forelegs reach straight and free from the shoulders, with elbows close. Hind legs to move in a straight line. Cowhocks or any suggestion of hind leg toeing in or out are faults.

Temperament—For all his diminutive size, the Maltese seems to be without fear. His trust and affectionate responsiveness are very appealing. He is among the gentlest mannered of all little dogs, yet he is lively and playful as well as vigorous.

The Standard for any breed is of greatest help to those who have raised dogs for some time, for they know what some of the less obvious terminology means. Interpretation of some of the phraseology is at times difficult for the novice in the breed. The description of general appearance and size presents no problems in analysis, but some of the other areas need to be clarified to prevent misinterpretation.

The shape of the head of the Maltese has gone through a gradual evolution during the last twenty to thirty years. This change, for the most part, is the result of the modification of the proportion of the muzzle to the total length of head. In the past, Maltese tended to have longer muzzles, frequently accounting for half the length of the head. This would, of course, give the head a much narrower shape and the balance of head to body would be quite different. This longer muzzled head is frequently referred to as a "Terrier head," and could well explain why there have been references to the Maltese Terrier in many publications in the past. If the muzzle length were to be held closer to one-third of the head length rather than to one-half, the dog would have a much softer expression, which would justify the classification of the Maltese as a Spaniel-type dog.

Not only is the length of muzzle important, but also its width in comparison to its length. An extremely narrow, or snipy muzzle, even though the overall length is correct, would tend to present an unbalanced picture.

This line sketch shows the correct body proportions of the Maltese according to the Standard. The heavy lines on the front and rear legs trace the bone pattern, showing shoulder placement and rear angulation.

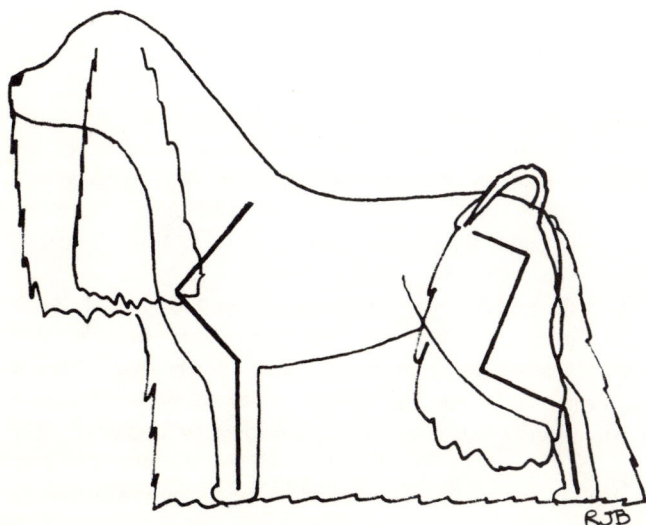

RJB

The skull, or that part of the head from the eye back, should be gently rounded. This will make possible a moderate stop where the skull meets the muzzle. The stop is that slight dip at the eye that prevents a straight line from being drawn flat along the profile between the occiput (at the upper back point of the skull) and the tip of the nose. The Collie head is representative of this straight line resting almost flat against the profile in comparison to the Pekingese whose stop is so severe that only the most exaggeratedly curved line could connect these two points of the head.

The Maltese is to be a compact dog and is frequently referred to as a square dog. This merely means that he is as long as he is tall. This statement may be somewhat deceptive, for the Standard says that he is square at the point of withers, or front shoulder. Since the dog extends beyond the withers, he will appear somewhat longer than he is tall. This is the correct balance for the Maltese; for if he were to appear perfectly square from the front of his chest to the base of his tail, he would really be taller on leg than he should be. This particular balance does exist in some Maltese and they are referred to as "leggy" dogs, meaning that their legs are too long for their bodies.

The topline is to be level. This means that the dog is as tall in the hindquarters as he is at the shoulders. The topline should slope neither up nor down from front to rear. The topline should not dip—a condition called sway-backed—nor should there be a hump. A hump in a dog's topline is called a "roach," and while it is acceptable in some breeds, it is not acceptable in the Maltese.

The ribs are to be well sprung. This indicates that the rib cage is to be larger than the loin area or the area immediately behind the ribs. This means that the chest would necessarily be fairly deep in comparison to the loin area and would result in a slight tuck-up. The tuck-up is the upward curve which starts at the end of the rib cage and continues to the rear quarters of the dog. On short-haired breeds, the tuck-up can easily be seen from a side view. On the long-haired breeds, the judge must feel this tuck-up with his hands, for it cannot be seen through the thick coat.

The tail of the Maltese must be carried up and over the back. The tail may rest directly on the back or lie to either side, allowing the long hair to cascade gently down the side of the dog. In the mature dog, the hair will be so long that it will reach to the floor. A tail that is set too low in relation to the topline will cause the tail to be carried higher than it should be and will not permit it to rest on the back. When this condition reaches an exaggerated point and the tail stands almost straight up, it is called a "gay tail." This is considered a very serious problem, for the trait is hereditary and will be passed on to succeeding generations. A dog with this condition should not be used in a breeding program.

When viewed from the front, the forelegs are to be parallel to each other. The radius and the ulna bones (the bones of the dog's forearm) should be straight. The joint between the radius and the humerus (that is, the elbow joint) should be set close to the body. When this is not the case, the dog is said to be "out at the elbows." This condition will result in the dog's being bowlegged if the feet are directly under the dog, or in his being too wide in front if the legs are straight and he is "out at the elbows."

The Maltese is to be moderately angulated in the rear. This means that when the dog is standing in a natural pose, his rear feet are not directly under his rear quarters, but are slightly to the rear of this position. There should be a gentle angling to the rear of both the stifle and the hock. The hock of the dog is made up of the metatarsal bones and is equivalent to the bottom of the foot in man. In the dog, however, the metatarsal bones do not rest flat on the floor, but, rather, are more or less perpendicular to it. In the Doberman Pinscher, for example, the hock is perpendicular to the floor. In the Maltese the angle should be approximately eighty-five degrees rather than ninety degrees. This will allow the dog to move smoothly with long, graceful strides. A dog that is straight in the stifles will not have the proper reach of movement in the rear quarters and will have a tendency to bounce when he gaits at even a moderate pace.

The center lines of the rear feet should be parallel to each other. This will cause the dog to move in a straight line. If the dog is cowhocked, the joints between the femur and the tibia (that is, the hock joints) angle toward each other when viewed from the rear. Being cowhocked will cause the feet to point outward and result in a hobble-like gait. If the feet point in, the dog is pigeon-toed and he will tend to have a rolling-type movement when viewed from the rear.

The perfect Maltese has not yet been bred. It is, therefore, necessary to weigh a dog's strong qualities against his weak ones. This is what the judge does at the show. He tries to pick the specimen with the most strong points and the fewest weak ones. The breed winner at a dog show is called the Best of Breed. He is just that. He is the best one entered that day, but not necessarily a perfect Maltese.

Ch. Maltacello's el Matador, owned by Delores Lewis and Maurine Middleton.

Best-in-Show Ch. Joanne-Chen's Maya Dancer and Handler Peggy A. Hogg.

The Maltese Personality

The diminutive show Maltese in an elegantly groomed, flowing white coat consistently captures the hearts of the ring-side spectators. It is almost impossible not to fall in love with such a little showman. His coat has the distinction of being absolutely white without any hint of a cream or yellow cast. He is, in reality, "squeaky" white.

His physical beauty is merely one of the qualities that endear him to all men. He has enough personality and unbounded energy to fill a two-hundred pound Saint Bernard. While it is the regal beauty of the Maltese that captures the fancy of the spectator, it is really his personality that is most highly treasured by those who own a Maltese.

The breed Standard states that "for all his diminutive size, the Maltese seems to be without fear. His trust and affectionate responsiveness are very appealing. He is among the gentlest mannered of all little dogs, yet he is lively and playful as well as vigorous." What the Standard really means is that the Maltese is a super-concentrated little bundle of energy which seems to have the ability to be in several places at the same time. In a roomful of people he appoints himself the official host and greeter, making every effort to ingratiate himself to all. He runs from one to another and seems to be able to detect the non-dog lover, on whom he lavishes special attention in an all-out effort to make him a believer.

It is difficult not to fall completely in love with this little white charmer. He is not in the least retiring and has the perseverance to get the attention of strangers as well as members of the family and to hold that attention until he has communicated whatever bit of information he wishes to share. This may mean that he wants to be taken for a walk, that he wants a drink, or that he merely wants to have a quiet little conversation with someone special. Whatever the motivation or the goal, he holds out tenaciously until he has his way.

The Maltese is a genuine little clown and a real theatrical ham. He knows well the value of the spotlight and a little publicity.

Several years ago there was a Best-in-Show Maltese who was a real professional in the ring. She knew that the judge was the one person she had to impress. She played to her audience, but she seemed to know that the win was really not made on that side of the fence. She was superbly well behaved while the judge was examining her, but her patience was just a little short when he was considering her competition. She tolerated the judge's attention to the competition just so long and then made her move. She gave two or three sharp little barks until the judge looked back her way. When she had his attention, she turned her head back and posed perfectly. She repeated this act whenever she felt it was necessary. This little act not only seemed to amuse the judges but brought bursts of applause from the spectators.

In addition to being a ham, a Maltese can be a devilish little imp as well. My own Ch. Good Time Hilda loved to go to shows. She was intrigued by the noise and the confusion and loved to have a stage on which she could show off. While she could be a real lady, she was a tomboy at heart. One day we were at an outside summer show at a fairgrounds. The day was moderately nice but there had been rain the night before and there were puddles in various low places in the rings. The gaiting area was, however, comparatively dry and the puddles could be avoided. On the first go-around, Hilda spotted a little puddle and tugged on the lead just enough to allow her to run through the one-inch deep water. I was aghast with the dripping dog at the other end of the lead. Hilda was delighted. It took careful control to avoid a repeat performance at each opportunity. Since the class was large and the day was warm, Hilda's patience grew a little short. While the judge was looking at several of the dogs milling on loose leads, Hilda bolted for the biggest mud hole, where she plopped down to cool off. She was obviously content with herself and not in the least offended that she did not receive further consideration from the judge.

Recently there was a very famous Best-in-Show winner who had a genuine dislike for liver. As a result, he was never baited by his handler. One day, after having won the Toy Group, he was back in the ring for the Best-in-Show judging. After the judge had gone over the Maltese, he reached down and picked up a piece of liver lying on the floor. He tried to bait the little dog with it. To show his displeasure with the liver, if not with the judge, the Maltese broke his pose and turned around to offer a rear view to the judge. He won in spite of his dislike for liver and his rudeness to the judge.

A most charming aspect of the Toy dog personality is seen when the puppy is a member of a family of Maltese. A litter of Maltese puppies romping in the back yard with their dam or older brothers and sisters is an exciting spectacle. They have unlimited amounts of energy. They seem to bounce and float rather than to walk or run. They look like big cotton balls tossed gently by the wind, and they seem to be everywhere at once. The older dogs are most tolerant and understanding of the challenging enthusiasm of the puppies. The puppies play until they are completely exhausted and then they suddenly drop down and take a brief nap just about anywhere. In a few minutes they wake up and seem to be completely refreshed, eager to start all over again.

In spite of the fact that most Maltese owners do not attempt to train their little dogs particularly, a Maltese is an extremely intelligent and easily trained dog. Most pet owners, however, are so intrigued by the antics of their puppy that they let him do whatever he wants to do. While the size makes this tolerable with a little dog, it is really improper not to train a dog and bring him at least to a minimal level of acceptable behavior. Complete obedience training is not necessary, but it can easily be accomplished. A number of owners of Maltese have elected to take their dogs through obedience training. While this has not been an extremely popular route because of the amount of work required of the owner, it is becoming more and more popular. There are a number of Maltese who have earned the Companion Dog (C.D.) degree and the Companion Dog Excellent (C.D.X.) degree. There are even a few who have won the difficult Utility Dog (U.D.) title. Spectators at the shows who are accustomed to seeing German Shepherds and Doberman Pinschers work in obedience are delighted with the little Maltese as he performs in the ring.

Snow Belle of
Shiraz, C.D.,
owned by Mrs.
Claudette LeMay.

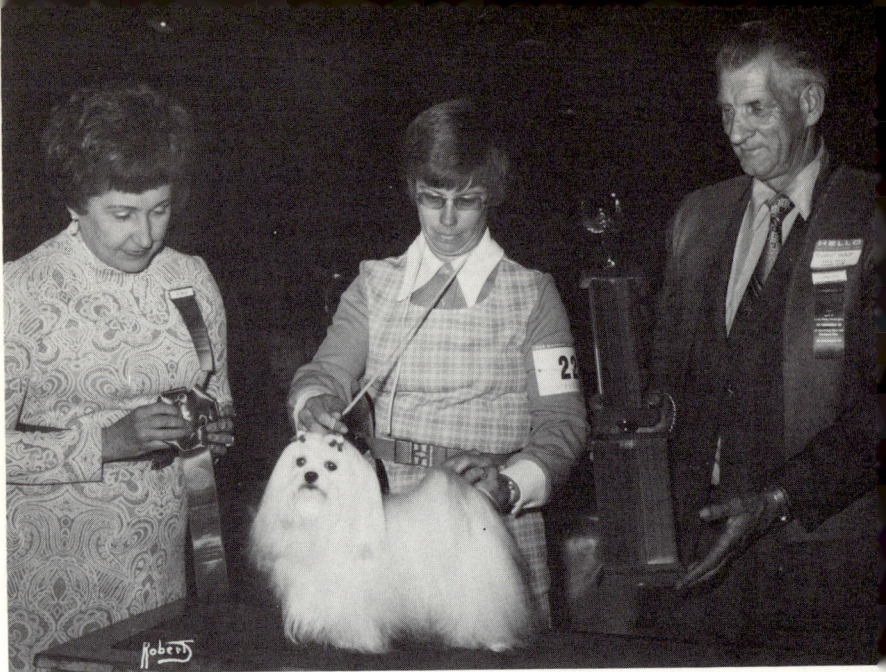

Ch. Al-Dor Pzazz, owned by Art and Grace Hendrickson.

Ch. Nyssamead's Chloe, owned by Susan M. Weber and Annette Feldblum.

Conditioning the Maltese

The conditioning of the Maltese is of prime importance both for his health and for his happiness. Because the basic diet of the dog is the key to proper conditioning, a well-balanced diet should be maintained at all times. Meals can be varied to make them interesting without sacrificing standards of nutrition, and vitamin and mineral supplements can be added.

Proper nutrition is necessary for a healthy coat. A dog cannot grow a proper coat unless he is fed a well-balanced diet. Before he can produce the quantity of coat he should have, he must gain and must maintain the weight consistent with his size.

In addition, proper exercise is necessary for all dogs. An hour or two each day should be set aside to exercise the dog. This can be accomplished by the owner's taking him for a walk, or by the dog's being allowed to romp in a fenced area. A well-drained dog run covered with three or four inches of gravel is easy to keep clean and will keep the dog out of the mud on rainy days. An occasional lime treatment eliminates odors. Dry lime can be sprinkled over the surface and then thoroughly washed through with a hose to prevent the dog's picking it up on the pads of his feet.

A clean exercise area helps keep the dog clean and prevents unnecessary bathing. Regular bathing does not hurt the dog's coat or health provided it is done with care. Show dogs are bathed at least once a week, and they are able to grow beautiful coats.

There are a number of good shampoos prepared especially for dogs, as well as creme rinses which can be applied after bathing to help control matting. But such products should be used with caution the first few times in order to determine the reaction of a particular dog. A thorough rinsing is extremely important, for all traces of soap and non-natural substances must be removed. The bathing process can be speeded up if the owner uses an electric dryer while brushing out the dog's coat.

The coat of the Maltese is one of its outstanding characteristics and the one that attracts the attention and interest of dog admirers everywhere. A Maltese with a neat, full coat is truly a remarkable example of the breed, while, in contrast, one whose coat has not been cared for is not only unattractive but also unsuccessful in the show ring.

Staining under the eyes is a problem with white dogs. Minor stains may be treated by rubbing Fuller's Earth into the hair while the hair is wet. After it has dried, the Fuller's Earth should be brushed out carefully. This treatment may be repeated. For more severe staining, boric acid powder may be used in place of Fuller's Earth.

A regular schedule of bathing and grooming should be established early in the puppy's life so that the owner is always well ahead of any coat problem that might arise. Brushing should start while the puppy is only a few weeks old. His coat will need very little serious attention at this early age, but the brushing will help train the puppy for some of the longer grooming sessions which will follow at a later date. The easiest way to start such training is for the owner to brush the coat gently while holding the puppy on his lap.

Sometime between the age of eight and ten months, a puppy will begin to lose his first coat. As the old hair falls out it will become matted in the new coat. This condition will require daily brushings for about a month until all the puppy coat has been shed.

A clean coat is a healthy coat. A coat that is allowed to become dirty will tangle quickly and will develop small mats which will either break the hair or cause it to be broken in working out the mat. If the coat is dirty or sticky or caked with mud, which is often the case when the dog is allowed to run freely in the yard, the dog should be bathed thoroughly before attempting to brush him. A partial bath or even a partial rinsing can save needless work and worry. It is to be remembered, however, that the hair is in its weakest condition when it is wet, and can be damaged easily.

With the proper training, the adult dog will lie still on his side on a table so that the underside can be groomed readily, and the groomer can use both hands in working on the stomach and under the legs where mats can develop rather quickly. Care must be taken to groom from the skin out. Many inexperienced groomers do not get out the tiny mats next to the skin, which destroy the outer coat as it becomes entangled.

With the dog lying on his side, the groomer should begin under the muzzle, pushing the hair back. Then gradually, layer by layer, he should line-brush the hair toward himself, using a large stainless steel pin brush. Large mats can be detected easily, but small mats are felt only by the pulling pressure of the brush. When mats are encountered, they should be worked out with the fingers or with a single tooth of a comb, pulling one hair loose at a time, if necessary, to avoid breaking the hairs.

When the groomer has covered a small section with the pin brush, he should go back over the same area with the slicker brush; but this should be done with great care, for the slicker brush will cut the hair if used improperly. When using the slicker brush, the groomer will discover new and even smaller mats, since the teeth of the slicker brush are set closer together. Again, these mats should be worked out carefully. The final step is to go over the same area a third time with a metal comb. This last step is important, for by the time the comb goes smoothly through the hair, the groomer can be sure that there are no mats left.

After completing the muzzle area, the groomer should move to the chest, the underside of the leg, and then to the outer side of the leg. After the groomer brushes the stomach and the lower side, and both sides of the rear leg, the dog should be turned on his stomach and the process repeated, moving from the head to the rear and line-brushing up to the part. With the dog still on his stomach, it will be easy to do the tail before moving to the other side and repeating the whole process again.

After grooming the dog a few times, the groomer will discover the ease of the technique and with practice the length of time required to brush the dog thoroughly and carefully will diminish. The regularity of brushing is of great importance in keeping the Maltese ready for the ring. With a regular grooming schedule, mats seldom develop and the dog will produce a coat of even length with healthy hair ends.

While grooming the dog, the groomer should use a little hair conditioner or water spray, which helps to cleanse foreign matter from hair ends and to prevent damage. Coats react differently to a given conditioner. It is wise, therefore, to experiment early on the puppy coat or on the underside of the dog in order to find the most successful spray for his texture of coat.

While a part in the hair down the middle of the back of the dog is natural, since hair that length has to fall to one side or the other, a straight line part is something that must be made by the groomer. The easiest way to get an even part after the dog is completely brushed is to use a knitting needle. Starting at the head and moving toward the tail, the groomer can part a two- or three-inch section at a time, sliding the needle down the backbone and then slowly drawing it up, allowing the hair to fall to either side. When the part is finished and straight, it should be sprayed with water the entire length in order to hold it.

Following the techniques and steps described above may be too time-consuming for the average pet owner. In this case it is kinder to the dog to keep his hair trimmed short, especially behind the ears and on the inside of the legs. He will not look like a show Maltese, but clipping him will eliminate the possibility of the hair's becoming so matted that it tears the skin and causes an infection.

To grow a "special's" coat on the Maltese, the coat must be wrapped. Groomers use different types of materials for this procedure, ranging from wax paper and plastic refrigerator wrap to nylon net. The latter, however, is a little too harsh for the Maltese coat.

The coat should be sprayed before wrapping it, using either water or a coat dressing. The topknots will be done in a single packet and held with a rubber band. Each side of the upper jaw whiskers will be held in a single packet, with the cheek whiskers in another packet. A single packet can contain the chin whiskers. Two or three packets, one above the other, will be needed for the front of the dog.

Depending on the density and the length of the side coat, the groomer will use either a single row of four packets or a double row, one being set high on the side and the other lower, to catch the hair on the underside. The front and back packets will be formed directly above the legs, while the coat in between will be held in two packets. Each side of the neck will require a single packet. The tail will be held in either one or two packets, depending on the length and thickness of the coat.

Getting the Maltese ready for the ring on the day of the show follows the bathing and pre-grooming the exhibitor did before leaving for the show. The coat must be meticulously groomed from the skin out so that there are no mats which will destroy the natural outline of the dog. By the time a dog is ready for the ring, he should have been thoroughly trained to lie on his side for whatever period of time is required to groom him completely. This training should be started months in advance so that the dog will not have to be disciplined the day of the show. The handler should avoid those actions which might make the dog nervous before he goes into the ring.

On the day of the show, the handler should groom the right side of the dog first, saving the "show side" for last. After each layer of brushing, the coat should be sprayed lightly with water or a diluted coat dressing to help keep the hair from flying and to keep it straight and in place for each succeeding layer.

After the dog has been completely brushed, he should be set up on the grooming table for the final treatment of the body part. After completing the body part, the groomer should return to the head to make the topknots. A horizontal part should be made from eye to eye, which will separate the hair that will be brushed down into the chin whiskers from that which will be brushed up to form the topknots.

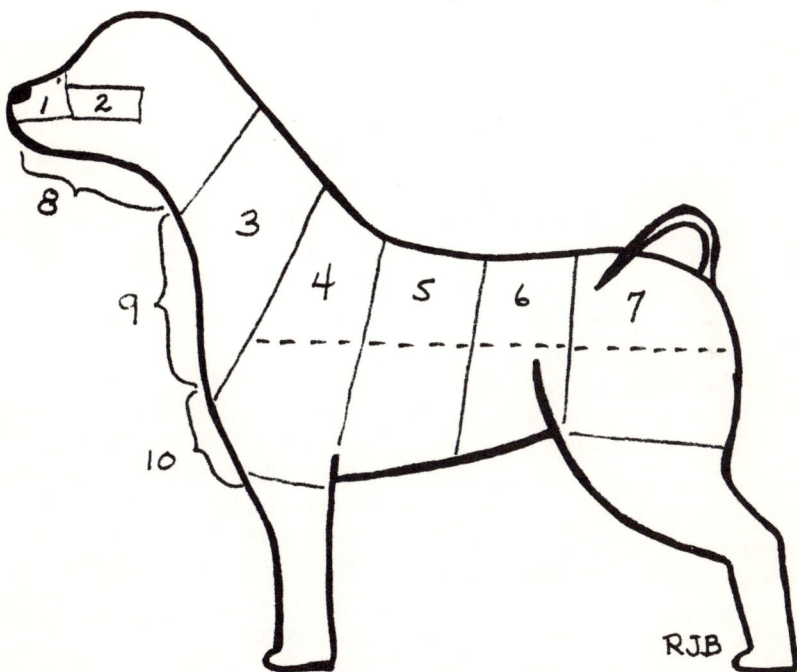

This line drawing shows how the hair should be parted for wrapping the show coat. Sections 4 through 7 can be divided at the dotted line if the coat is extremely dense or long.

The width of the two topknots is determined by the size of the head. Each will run from the center part to the outside corner of the eye and should be square. The outer top corners may be rounded slightly. This hair will be gathered and held in place with a white dental rubber band. The rubber band will be placed over the inside corner of the eye and at a height equivalent to two-thirds of the distance between the centers of the two eyes. This gives a very nice balance to the head and takes into consideration differences in head shapes. The lower portion of the topknot should be poufed out gently with the tooth of a comb before the remainder is folded back and held with a final twist of the rubber band. The final touch is to add the bows, which should be between one-half and three-quarters of an inch long, depending on the size of the head of the dog. Care must be taken to make sure that both topknots are the same size and shape and that the bows are placed evenly.

When the class is called, the handler should already have determined where his dog will show to the best advantage, and he should try to get in that place in line if he can accomplish it tactfully. If the dog gaits rapidly, the head of the line would be the preferred position. If the dog moves slowly, however, the end of the line is the obvious choice. A slow moving dog in the middle of the line only calls attention to the fact that he does not move well. The end of the line is also the best place to show the dog that keeps looking back at the dog following him. The handler should take advantage of those techniques which will show his dog to its best advantage. It should be remembered, however, that a competent judge will find the best dog no matter where he is in line as long as he is shown to advantage.

In the ring, the dog should be set up and then worked just enough to keep him in pose. Over-handling a dog tends to make him nervous and prevents the judge from getting a good look at him. The handler should remember that a judge is always looking at his dog. Even if a judge is at the other end of the line, he may glance back to see how another dog looks in comparison to the one he is examining. Allowing a dog to sit or sag can lose a placement.

Obviously, there is no perfect dog, for every dog has strong points and weak points. The strong points consequently should be emphasized and the weak ones minimized. Since the judge will pick the best dog in the class, the exhibitor must prove to him that his dog has more strong qualities than the other dogs in the ring. The judge will select the best one present that particular day in comparison with the other entries.

30

A show dog in coat wraps.

Professional Handler Dorothy White and Ch. Maltacello's Issa of Buckeye, ready for the Group ring. Owners are Mr. & Mrs. William P. Marsland.

Best-in-Show Ch. Aennchen's Paris Dancer, owned by Dr. & Mrs. Kenneth Knopf.

Grooming and
General Coat Care

Although coat types, textures, and patterns may seem purely arbitrary matters of little consequence, they are among the important characteristics that distinguish one breed from another. Actually, each breed has been developed to serve a specific purpose, and the coat that is considered typical for the breed is also the one most appropriate for the dog's specialized use—be it as guard, hunting companion, herder, or pet. A knowledge of the breed Standard approved by The American Kennel Club is helpful to the owner who takes pride in owning a well-groomed dog, typical of its breed.

Dogs with short, smooth coats (such as the Weimaraner, Basset, Beagle, smooth Dachshund and Chihuahua) usually shed only moderately and their coats require little routine grooming other than thorough brushing with a bristle brush or hound glove. For exhibition in the show ring, the whiskers, or "feelers," are trimmed close to the muzzle, but no other trimming is needed.

The wire coat of the Airedale, Wire Fox Terrier, Miniature Schnauzer, or Wirehaired Dachshund should be stripped or plucked in show trim at regular intervals. The dog can then be kept well groomed by thorough combing and brushing.

Curly coated breeds such as the Curly Coated Retriever, and the American and Irish Water Spaniels, generally require no special coat care other than frequent brushing. True curly coated breeds are very curly indeed and are not to be confused with breeds such as the Golden Retriever, Gordon Setter, Brittany Spaniel, and English Springer Spaniel, which have slightly curled or wavy coats of somewhat silky texture. The longer hair, or "feathers," typically found on tail, legs, ears, and chest of these breeds should be trimmed slightly to make the outline neater.

(UPPER LEFT) Wire brush (RIGHT) Bristle brush
(LOWER LEFT) Comb—Hound glove.

They are not "trimmed to pattern," however, as are such long-haired breeds as the Kerry Blue Terrier and the Poodle, which, when shown in the breed ring, must be clipped and trimmed in the patterns specified in the breed Standards.

The Longhaired Dachshund, the Borzoi, and the Yorkshire Terrier have long but comparatively silky coats, whereas the Newfoundland and the Rough Collie have long straight coats with rather harsh texture. Long coats must be kept brushed out thoroughly to eliminate mats and snarls.

The dog should be taught from puppyhood that a grooming session is a time for business, not for play. He should be handled gently, though, for it is essential to avoid hurting him in any way. Grooming time should be pleasant for both dog and master.

Tools required vary with the breed, but always include combs, brushes, and nail clippers and files. Combs should have wide-spaced teeth with rounded ends so that the dog's skin will not be scratched accidentally. For the same reason, brushes with natural bristles are usually preferable to those with synthetic bristles that may be too fine and sharp.

A light, airy, pleasant place in which to work is desirable, and it is of the utmost importance that neither dog nor master be distracted by other dogs, cats, or people. Consequently, it is usually preferable that grooming be done indoors.

Particularly for large or medium breeds, a sturdy grooming table is desirable. Many owners hold small puppies or Toy dogs during grooming sessions, athough it is better if they, too, are groomed on a table. Large and medium size dogs should be taught to jump onto the table and to jump off again when grooming is completed. Small dogs must be lifted on and off to avoid falls and possible injury. The dog should stand while the back and upper portions of the body are groomed, and lie on his side while underparts of his body are brushed, nails clipped, etc.

Before each session, the dog should be permitted to relieve himself. Once grooming is begun, it is important to avoid keeping the dog standing so long that he becomes tired. If a good deal of grooming is needed, it should be done in two or more short periods.

It is almost impossible to brush too much, and show dogs are often brushed for a full half hour a day, year round. If you cannot brush your dog every day, you should brush him a minimum of two or three times a week. Brushing removes loose skin particles and stimulates circulation, thereby improving condition of the skin. It also stimulates secretion of the natural skin oils that make the coat look healthy and beautiful.

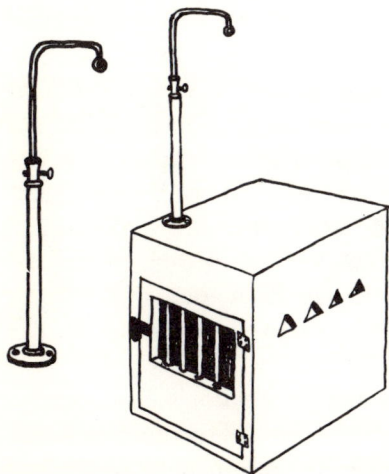

Dog crate with grooming—table top is ideal—providing rigid, well supported surface on which to groom dog, and serving as indoor kennel for puppy or grown dog. Rubber matting provides non-slip surface. Dog's collar may be attached to adjustable arm. Lightweight and readily transported yet sturdy, the crate is especially useful to owner who takes dog with him when he travels.

Before brushing, any burs adhering to the coat, as well as matted hair, should be carefully removed, using the fingers and coarse toothed comb with a gentle, teasing motion to avoid tearing the coat. The coat should first be brushed lightly in the direction in which the hair grows. Next, it should be brushed vigorously in the opposite direction, a small portion at a time, making sure the bristles penetrate the hair to the skin, until the entire coat has been brushed thoroughly and all loose soil removed. Then the coat should be brushed in the direction the hair grows, until every hair is sleekly in place.

The dog that is kept well brushed needs bathing only rarely. Once or twice a year is usually enough. Except for unusual circumstances when his coat becomes excessively soiled, no puppy under six months of age should be bathed in water. If it is necessary to bathe a puppy, extreme care must be exercised so that he will not become chilled. No dog should be bathed during cold weather and then permitted to go outside immediately. Whatever the weather, the dog should always be given a good run outdoors and permitted to relieve himself before he is bathed.

Various types of "dry baths" are available at pet supply stores. In general, they are quite satisfactory when circumstances are such that a bath in water is impractical. Dry shampoos are usually rubbed into the dog's coat thoroughly, then removed by vigorous towelling or brushing.

Before starting a water bath, the necessary equipment should be assembled. This includes a tub of appropriate size, and another tub or pail for rinse water. (A small hose with a spray nozzle— one that may be attached to the water faucet—is ideal for rinsing the dog.) A metal or plastic cup for dipping water, special dog shampoo, a small bottle of mineral or olive oil, and a supply of absorbent cotton should be placed nearby, as well as a supply of heavy towels, a wash cloth, and the dog's combs and brushes.

The amount of water required will vary according to the size of the dog, but should reach no higher than the dog's elbows. Bath water and rinse water should be slightly warmer than lukewarm, but should not be hot.

To avoid accidentally getting water in the dog's ears, place a small amount of absorbent cotton in each. With the dog standing in the tub, wet his body by using the cup to pour water over him. Take care to avoid wetting the head, and be careful to avoid getting water or shampoo in the eyes. (If you should accidentally do so, placing a few drops of mineral or olive oil in the inner corner of the eye will bring relief.) When the dog is thoroughly wet, put a small amount of shampoo on his back and work up a lather, rubbing briskly. Wash his entire body and then rinse as much of the shampoo as possible from the coat by dipping water from the tub and pouring it over the dog.

Dip the wash cloth into clean water, wring it out enough so it won't drip, then wash the dog's head, taking care to avoid the eyes. Remove the cotton from the dog's ears and sponge them gently, inside and out. Shampoo should never be used inside the ears, so if they are extremely soiled, sponge them clean with cotton saturated with mineral or olive oil. (Between baths, the ears should be cleaned frequently in the same way.)

Replace the cotton in the ears, then use the cup and container of rinse water (or hose and spray nozzle) to rinse the dog thoroughly. Quickly wrap a towel around him, remove him from the tub, and towel him as dry as possible. To avoid getting an impromptu bath yourself, you must act quickly, for once he is out of the tub, the dog will instinctively shake himself.

While the hair is still slightly damp, use a clean comb or brush to remove any tangles. If the hair is allowed to dry first, it may be completely impossible to remove them.

So far as routine grooming is concerned, the dog's eyes require little attention. Some dogs have a slight accumulation of mucus in the corner of the eyes upon waking mornings. A salt solution (1 teaspoon of table salt to one pint of warm, sterile water) can be sponged around the eyes to remove the stain. During grooming sessions it is well to inspect the eyes, since many breeds are prone to eye injury. Eye problems of a minor nature may be treated at home (see page 50), but it is imperative that any serious eye abnormality be called to the attention of the veterinarian immediately.

Feeding hard dog biscuits and hard bones helps to keep tooth surfaces clean. Slight discoloration may be readily removed by rubbing with a damp cloth dipped in salt or baking soda. The dog's head should be held firmly, the lips pulled apart gently, and the teeth rubbed lightly with the dampened cloth. Regular

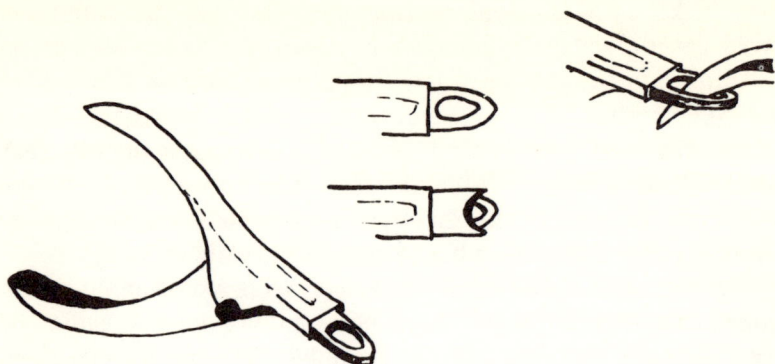

Nail trimmer—center detail shows blade cutting action. Right shows manner of inserting nail in cutter.

care usually keeps the teeth in good condition, but if tartar accumulates, it should be removed by a veterinarian.

If the dog doesn't keep his nails worn down through regular exercise on hard surfaces, they must be trimmed at intervals, for nails that are too long may cause the foot to spread and thus spoil the dog's gait. Neglected nails may even grow so long that they will grow into a circle and puncture the dog's skin. Nails can be cut easily with a nail trimmer that slides over the nail end. The cut is made just outside the faintly pink bloodline that can be seen on white nails. In pigmented nails, the bloodline is not easily seen, so the cut should be made just outside the hooklike projection on the underside of the nails. A few downward strokes with a nail file will smooth the cut surface, and, once shortened, nails can be kept short by filing at regular intervals.

Care must be taken that nails are not cut too short, since blood vessels may be accidentally severed. Should you accidentally cut a nail so short that it bleeds, apply a mild antiseptic and keep the dog quiet until bleeding stops. Usually, only a few drops of blood will be lost. But once a dog's nails have been cut painfully short, he will usually object when his feet are handled.

Nutrition

The main food elements required by dogs are proteins, fats, and carbohydrates. Vitamins A, B complex, D, and E are essential, as are ample amounts of calcium and iron. Nine other minerals are required in small amounts but are amply provided in almost any diet, so there is no need to be concerned about them.

The most important nutrient is protein and it must be provided every day of the dog's life, for it is essential for normal daily growth and replacement of body tissues burned up in daily activity. Preferred animal protein products are beef, mutton, horse meat, and boned fish. Visceral organs—heart, liver, and tripe—are good but if used in too large quantities may cause diarrhea (bones in large amounts have the same effect). Pork, particularly fat pork, is undesirable. The "meat meal" used in some commercial foods is made from scrap meat processed at high temperatures and then dried. It is not quite so nutritious as fresh meat, but in combination with other protein products, it is an acceptable ingredient in the dog's diet.

Cooked eggs and raw egg yolk are good sources of protein, but raw egg white should never be fed since it cannot be digested by the dog and may cause diarrhea. Cottage cheese and milk (fresh, dried, and canned) are high in protein, also. Puppies thrive on milk and it can well be included in the diet of older dogs, too, if mixed with meat, vegetables, and meal. Soy-bean meal, wheat germ meal, and dried brewers yeast are vegetable products high in protein and may be used to advantage in the diet.

Vegetable and animal fats in moderate amounts should be used, especially if a main ingredient of the diet is dry or kibbled food. Fats should not be used excessively or the dog may become overweight. Generally, fats should be increased slightly in the winter and reduced somewhat during warm weather.

Carbohydrates are required for proper assimilation of fats. Dog biscuits, kibble, dog meal, and other dehydrated foods are good sources of carbohydrates, as are cereal products derived from rice, corn, wheat, and ground or rolled oats.

Vegetables supply additional proteins, vitamins, and minerals, and by providing bulk are of value in overcoming constipation. Raw or cooked carrots, celery, lettuce, beets, asparagus, tomatoes, and cooked spinach may be used. They should always be chopped or ground well and mixed with the other food. Various combinations may be used, but a good home-mixed ration for the mature dog consists of two parts of meat and one each of vegetables and dog meal (or cereal product).

Dicalcium phosphate and cod-liver oil are added to puppy diets to ensure inclusion of adequate amounts of calcium and Vitamins A and D. Indiscriminate use of dietary supplements is not only unjustified but may actually be harmful and many breeders feel that their over-use in diets of extremely small breeds may lead to excessive growth as well as to overweight at maturity.

Foods manufactured by well-known and reputable food processors are nutritionally sound and are offered in sufficient variety of flavors, textures, and consistencies that most dogs will find them tempting and satisfying. Canned foods are usually "ready to eat," while dehydrated foods in the form of kibble, meal, or biscuits may require the addition of water or milk. Dried foods containing fat sometimes become rancid, so to avoid an unpalatable change in flavor, the manufacturer may not include fat in dried food but recommend its addition at the time the water or milk is added.

Candy and other sweets are taboo, for the dog has no nutritional need for them and if he is permitted to eat them, he will usually eat less of foods he requires. Also taboo are fried foods, highly seasoned foods and extremely starchy foods, for the dog's digestive tract is not equipped to handle them.

Frozen foods should be thawed completely and warmed at least to lukewarm, while hot foods should be cooled to lukewarm. Food should be in a fairly firm state, for sloppy food is difficult for the dog to digest.

Whether meat is raw or cooked makes little difference, so long as the dog is also given the juice that seeps from the meat during cooking. Bones provide little nourishment, although gnawing bones helps make the teeth strong and helps to keep tartar from accumulating on them. Beef bones, especially large knuckle bones, are best. Fish, poultry, and chop bones should never be given to dogs since they have a tendency to splinter and may puncture the dog's digestive tract.

Clean, fresh, cool water is essential to all dogs and an adequate supply should be readily available twenty-four hours a day from the time the puppy is big enough to walk. Especially during hot weather, the drinking pan should be emptied and refilled at frequent intervals.

Puppies usually are weaned by the time they are six weeks old, so when you acquire a new puppy ten to twelve weeks old, he will already have been started on a feeding schedule. The breeder should supply exact details as to number of meals per day, types and amounts of food offered, etc. It is essential to adhere to this established routine, for drastic changes in diet may produce intestinal upsets.

Until a puppy is six months old, milk formula is an integral part of the diet. A day's supply should be made up at one time and stored in the refrigerator, and the quantity needed for each meal warmed at feeding time. The following combination is good for all breeds:

1 pint whole fresh milk	1 tablespoon lime water
1 raw egg yolk, slightly beaten	1 tablespoon lactose

The two latter items (as well as cod-liver oil and dicalcium phosphate to be added to solid food) are readily available at pet supply stores and drug stores.

At twelve weeks of age the amount of formula given at each feeding will vary from three to four tablespoonfuls for the Toy breeds, to perhaps two cupfuls for the large breeds. If the puppy is on the five-meal-a-day schedule when he leaves the kennel, three of the meals (first, third, and fifth each day) should consist of formula only. On a four-meal schedule, the first and fourth meals should be formula.

In either case, the second meal of the day should consist of chopped beef (preferably raw). The amount needed will vary from about three tablespoonfuls for Toy breeds up to one-half cupful for large breeds. The other meal should consist of equal parts of chopped beef and strained, cooked vegetables to which is added a little dry toast. (If you plan eventually to feed your dog canned food or dog meal, it can gradually be introduced at this meal.) Cod-liver oil and dicalcium phosphate should be mixed with the food for this meal. The amount of each will vary from one-half teaspoonful for Toys to 1 tablespoonful for large breeds.

The amount of food offered at each meal must gradually be increased and by five months the puppy will require about twice what he needed at three months. Puppies should be fat, and it is best to let them eat as much as they want at each meal, so long as they are hungry again when it is time for the next feeding. Any food not eaten within fifteen minutes should be taken away. With a little attention to the dog's eating habits, the owner can prepare enough food and still not waste any.

When the puppy is five months old, the final feeding of the day can be eliminated and the five meals compressed into four so the puppy still receives the same quantities and types of food. At six or seven months, the four meals can be compressed into three. By the time a puppy of small or medium breed is eleven to twelve months old, feedings can be reduced to two meals a day. At the end of the first year, cod-liver oil and dicalcium phosphate can usually be discontinued.

Large breeds mature more slowly and three meals a day are usually necessary until eighteen or twenty-four months of age. Cod-liver oil and dicalcium phosphate should be continued, too, until the large dog reaches maturity.

A mature dog usually eats slightly less than he did as a growing puppy. For mature dogs, one large meal a day is usually sufficient, although some owners prefer to give two meals. As long as the dog enjoys optimum health and is neither too fat nor too thin, the number of meals a day makes little difference.

The amount of food required for mature dogs will vary. With canned dog food or home-prepared foods (that is, the combination of meat, vegetables, and meal), the approximate amount required is one-half ounce of food per pound of body weight. Thus, about eight ounces of such foods would be needed each day for a mature dog weighing sixteen pounds. If the dog is fed a dehydrated commercial food, approximately one ounce of food is needed for each pound of body weight. Approximately one pound of dry food per day would be required by a dog weighing sixteen pounds. Most manufacturers of commercial foods provide information on packages as to approximate daily needs of various breeds.

As a dog becomes older and less active, he may become too fat. Or his appetite may decrease so he becomes too thin. It is necessary to adjust the diet in either case, for the dog will live longer and enjoy better health if he is maintained in trim condition. The simplest way to decrease or increase body weight is by decreasing or increasing the amount of fat in the diet. Protein content should be maintained at a high level throughout the dog's life, although the amount of food at each meal can be decreased if the dog becomes too fat.

If the older dog becomes reluctant to eat, it may be necessary to coax him with special food he normally relishes. Warming the food will increase its aroma and usually will help to entice the dog to eat. If he still refuses, rubbing some of the food on the dog's lips and gums may stimulate interest. It may be helpful also to offer food in smaller amounts and increase the number of meals per day. Foods that are highly nutritious and easily digested are especially desirable for older dogs. Small amounts of cooked, ground liver, cottage cheese, or mashed, hard-cooked eggs should be included in the diet often.

Before a bitch is bred, her owner should make sure that she is in optimum condition—slightly on the lean side rather than fat. The bitch in whelp is given much the same diet she was fed prior to breeding, with slight increases in amounts of meat, liver, and dairy products. Beginning about six weeks after breeding, she should be fed two meals per day rather than one, and the total daily intake increased. (Some bitches in whelp require as much as 50% more food than they consume normally.) She must not be permitted to become fat, for whelping problems are more likely to occur in overweight dogs. Cod-liver oil and dicalcium phosphate should be provided until after the puppies are weaned. The amount of each will vary from one-half teaspoonful to one tablespoonful a day, depending upon her size.

The dog used only occasionally for breeding will not require a special diet, but he should be well fed and maintained in optimum condition. A dog that is at public stud and used frequently may require a slightly increased amount of food. But his basic diet will require no change so long as his general health is good and his flesh is firm and hard.

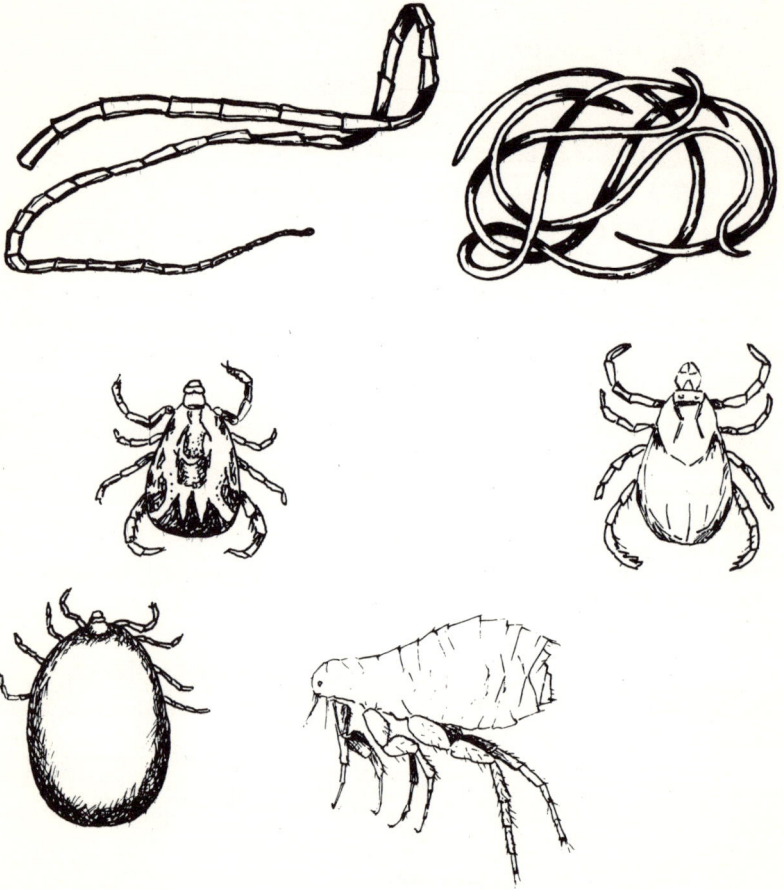

Some common internal and external parasites.

(UPPER LEFT) Tape worm. (UPPER RIGHT) Round worms. (CENTER) American dog ticks—left, female and right, male (much enlarged). (LOWER LEFT) Female tick engorged. (LOWER RIGHT) dog flea (much enlarged).

Maintaining the Dog's Health

Proper nutrition is essential in maintaining the dog's resistance to infectious diseases, in reducing susceptibility to organic diseases, and, of course, in preventing dietary deficiency diseases.

Rickets is probably the most common deficiency disease and afflicts puppies not provided sufficient calcium and Vitamin D. Bones fail to calcify properly, development of teeth is retarded, joints become knobby and deformed, and muscles are flabby. Symptoms include lameness, arching of neck and back, and a tendency of the legs to bow. Treatment consists of providing adequate amounts of dicalcium phosphate and Vitamin D and exposing the dog to sunlight. If detected and treated before reaching an advanced stage, bone damage may be lessened somewhat, although it cannot be corrected completely.

Osteomalacia, similar to rickets, may occur in adult dogs. Treatment is the same as for rickets, but here, too, prevention is preferable to cure. Permanent deformities resulting from rickets or osteomalacia will not be inherited, so once victims recover, they can be used for breeding.

To prevent the growth of disease-producing bacteria and other micro-organisms, cleanliness is essential. All equipment, especially water and food dishes, must be kept immaculately clean. Cleanliness is also essential in controlling external parasites, which thrive in unsanitary surroundings.

Fleas, lice, mites, and ticks can be eradicated in the dog's quarters by regular use of one of the insecticide sprays with a four to six weeks' residual effect. Bedding, blankets, and pillows should be laundered frequently and treated with an insecticide containing rotenone or DDT. Treatment for external parasites varies, depending upon the parasite involved, but a number of good dips and powders are available at pet stores.

Fleas may be eliminated by using a flea powder containing lindane. The coat must be dusted thoroughly with the powder at frequent intervals during the summer months when fleas are a problem. For eradicating lice, dips containing rotenone or DDT must be applied to the coat. A fine-toothed comb should then be used to remove dead lice and eggs, which are firmly attached to the coat. Mites live deep in the ear canal, producing irritation to the lining of the ear and causing a brownish-black, dry type discharge. Plain mineral oil or ear ointment should be swabbed on the inner surface of the ear twice a week until mites are eliminated. Ticks may carry Rocky Mountain spotted fever, so, to avoid possible infection, they should be removed from the dog only with tweezers and should be destroyed by burning (or by dropping them into insecticide). Heavy infestation can be controlled by sponging the coat daily with a solution containing a special tick dip.

Among preparations available for controlling parasites on the dog's body are some that can be given internally. Since dosage must be carefully controlled, these preparations should not be used without consulting a veterinarian.

Internal parasites, with the exception of the tapeworm, may be transmitted from a mother dog to the puppies. Infestation may also result from contact with infected bedding or through access to a yard where an infected dog relieves himself. The types that may infest dogs are roundworms, whipworms, tapeworms, hookworms, and heartworms. All cause similar symptoms: a generally unthrifty appearance, stary coat, dull eyes, weakness and emaciation despite a ravenous appetite, coughing, vomiting, diarrhea, and sometimes bloody stools. Not all symptoms are present in every case, of course.

Promiscuous dosing for worms is dangerous and different types of worms require different treatment. So if you suspect your dog has worms, ask your veterinarian to make a microscopic examination of the feces, and to prescribe appropriate treatment if evidence of worm infestation is found.

Clogged anal glands cause intense discomfort, which the dog may attempt to relieve by scooting himself along the floor on his haunches. These glands, located on either side of the anus, secrete a substance that enables the dog to expel the contents of the rectum. If they become clogged, they may give the dog an unpleasant odor and when neglected, serious infection may result. Contents of the glands can be easily expelled into a wad of

cotton, which should be held under the tail with the left hand. Then, using the right hand, pressure should be exerted with the thumb on one side of the anus, the forefinger on the other. The normal secretion is brownish in color, with an unpleasant odor. The presence of blood or pus indicates infection and should be called to the attention of a veterinarian.

Fits, often considered a symptom of worms, may result from a variety of causes, including vitamin deficiencies, or playing to the point of exhaustion. A veterinarian should be consulted when a fit occurs, for it may be a symptom of serious illness.

Distemper takes many and varied forms, so it is sometimes difficult for even experienced veterinarians to diagnose. It is the number one killer of dogs, and although it is not unknown in older dogs, its victims are usually puppies. While some dogs do recover, permanent damage to the brain or nervous system is often sustained. Symptoms may include lethargy, diarrhea, vomiting, reduced appetite, cough, nasal discharge, inflammation of the eyes, and a rise in temperature. If distemper is suspected, a veterinarian must be consulted at once, for early treatment is essential. Effective preventive measures lie in inoculation. Shots for temporary immunity should be given all puppies within a few weeks after whelping, and the permanent inoculations should be given as soon thereafter as possible.

Hardpad has been fairly prevalent in Great Britain for a number of years, and its incidence in the United States is increasing. Symptoms are similar to those of distemper, but as the disease progresses, the pads of the feet harden and eventually peel. Chances of recovery are not favorable unless prompt veterinary care is secured.

Infectious hepatitis in dogs affects the liver, as does the human form, but apparently is not transmissible to man. Symptoms are similar to those of distemper, and the disease rapidly reaches the acute stage. Since hepatitis is often fatal, prompt veterinary treatment is essential. Effective vaccines are available and should be provided all puppies. A combination distemper-hepatitis vaccine is sometimes used.

Leptospirosis is caused by a micro-organism often transmitted by contact with rats, or by ingestion of food contaminated by rats. The disease can be transmitted to man, so anyone caring for an afflicted dog must take steps to avoid infection. Symptoms include vomiting, loss of appetite, diarrhea, fever, depression and lethargy, redness of eyes and gums, and sometimes jaundice. Since permanent kidney damage may result, veterinary treatment should be secured immediately.

Rabies is a disease that is always fatal—and it is transmissible to man. It is caused by a virus that attacks the nervous system and is present in the saliva of an infected animal. When an infected animal bites another, the virus is transmitted to the new victim. It may also enter the body through cuts and scratches that come in contact with saliva containing the virus.

All warm-blooded animals are subject to rabies and it may be transmitted by foxes, skunks, squirrels, horses, and cattle as well as dogs. Anyone bitten by a dog (or other animal) should see his physician immediately, and health and law enforcement officials should be notified. Also, if your dog is bitten by another animal, consult your veterinarian immediately.

In most areas, rabies shots are required by law. Even if not required, all dogs should be given anti-rabies vaccine, for it is an effective preventive measure.

Injuries of a serious nature—deep cuts, broken bones, severe burns, etc.—always require veterinary care. However, the dog may need first aid before being moved to a veterinary hospital.

A dog injured in any way should be approached cautiously, for reactions of a dog in pain are unpredictable and he may bite even a beloved master. A muzzle should always be applied before any attempt is made to move the dog or treat him in any way. The muzzle can be improvised from a strip of cloth, bandage, or even heavy cord, looped firmly around the dog's jaws and tied under the lower jaw. The ends should then be extended back of the neck and tied again so the loop around the jaws will stay in place.

A stretcher for moving a heavy dog can be improvised from a rug or board—preferably two people should be available to transport it. A small dog can be carried by one person simply by grasping the loose skin at the nape of the neck with one hand and placing the other hand under the dog's hips.

Severe bleeding from a leg can be controlled by applying a tourniquet between the wound and the body, but the tourniquet must be loosened at ten-minute intervals. Severe bleeding from head or body can be controlled by placing a cloth or gauze pad over the wound, then applying firm pressure with the hand.

To treat minor cuts, first trim the hair from around the wound, then wash the area with warm soapy water and apply a mild antiseptic such as tincture of metaphen.

Shock is usually the aftermath of severe injury and requires immediate veterinary attention. The dog appears dazed, lips and tongue are pale, and breathing is shallow. The dog should be wrapped in blankets and kept warm, and if possible, kept lying down with his head lower than his body.

Fractures require immediate professional attention. A broken bone should be immobilized while the dog is transported to the veterinarian but no attempt should be made to splint it.

Burns from hot liquid or hot metals should be treated by applying a bland ointment, provided the burned area is small. Burns over large areas should be treated by a veterinarian.

Burns from chemicals should first be treated by flushing the coat with plain water, taking care to protect the dog's eyes and ears. A baking soda solution can then be applied to neutralize the chemical further. If the burned area is small, a bland ointment should be applied. If the burned area is large, more extensive treatment will be required, as well as veterinary care.

49

Poisoning is more often accidental than deliberate, but whichever the case, symptoms and treatment are the same. If the poisoning is not discovered immediately, the dog may be found unconscious. His mouth will be slimy, he will tremble, have difficulty breathing, and possibly go into convulsions. Veterinary treatment must be secured immediately.

If you find the dog eating something you know to be poisonous, induce vomiting immediately by repeatedly forcing the dog to swallow a mixture of equal parts of hydrogen peroxide and water. Delay of even a few minutes may result in death. When the contents of the stomach have been emptied, force the dog to swallow raw egg white, which will slow absorption of the poison. Then call the veterinarian. Provide him with information as to the type of poison, and follow his advice as to further treatment.

Some chemicals are toxic even though not swallowed, so before using a product, make sure it can be used safely around pets.

Electric shock usually results because an owner negligently leaves an electric cord exposed where the dog can chew on it. If possible, disconnect the cord before touching the dog. Otherwise, yank the cord from the dog's mouth so you will not receive a shock when you try to help him. If the dog is unconscious, artificial respiration and stimulants will be required, so a veterinarian should be consulted at once.

Eye problems of a minor nature—redness or occasional discharge—may be treated with a few drops of boric acid solution (2%) or salt solution (1 teaspoonful table salt to 1 pint sterile water). Cuts on the eyeball, bruises close to the eyes, or persistent discharge shoud be treated only by a veterinarian.

Skin problems usually cause persistent itching. However, *follicular mange* does not usually do so but is evidenced by moth-eaten-looking patches, especially about the head and along the back. *Sarcoptic mange* produces severe itching and is evidenced by patchy, crusty areas on body, legs, and abdomen. Any evidence suggesting either should be called to the attention of a veterinarian. Both require extensive treatment and both may be contracted by humans.

Eczema is characterized by extreme itching, redness of the skin and exudation of serous matter. It may result from a variety of causes, and the exact cause in a particular case may be difficult to determine. Relief may be secured by dusting the dog twice a week with a soothing powder containing a fungicide and an insecticide.

Allergies are not readily distinguished from other skin troubles except through laboratory tests. However, dog owners should be alert to the fact that straw, shavings, or newspapers used for bedding, various coat dressings and shampoos, or simply bathing the dog too often, may produce allergic skin reactions in some dogs. Thus, a change in dog-keeping practices often relieves them.

Symptoms of illness may be so obvious there is no question that the dog is ill, or so subtle that the owner isn't sure whether there is a change from normal or not. *Loss of appetite, malaise* (general lack of interest in what is going on), *and vomiting* may be ignored if they occur singly and persist only for a day. However, in combination with other evidence of illness, such symptoms may be significant and the dog should be watched closely. *Abnormal bowel movements,* especially diarrhea or bloody stools, are cause for immediate concern. *Urinary abnormalities* may indicate infections, and bloody urine is always an indication of a serious condition. When a dog that has long been housebroken suddenly becomes incontinent, a veterinarian should be consulted, for he may be able to suggest treatment or medication that will be helpful.

Persistent coughing is often considered a symptom of worms, but may also indicate heart trouble—especially in older dogs.

Vomiting is another symptom often attributed to worm infestation. Dogs suffering from indigestion sometimes eat grass, apparently to induce vomiting and relieve discomfort.

Stary coat—dull and lackluster—indicates generally poor health and possible worm infestation. *Dull eyes* may result from similar conditions. Certain forms of blindness may also cause the eyes to lose the sparkle of vibrant good health.

Fever is a positive indication of illness and consistent deviation from the normal temperature range of 100 to 102 degrees is cause for concern. To take the dog's temperature, first place the dog on his side. Coat the bulb of a rectal thermometer with petroleum jelly, raise the dog's tail, insert the thermometer to approximately half its length, and hold it in position for two minutes. Clean the thermometer with rubbing alcohol after each use and be sure to shake it down.

A dog that is seriously ill, requiring surgical treatment, transfusions, or intravenous feeding, must be hospitalized. One requiring less complicated treatment is better cared for at home, but it is essential that the dog be kept in a quiet environment. Preferably, his bed should be in a room apart from family activity, yet close at hand, so his condition can be checked frequently. Clean bedding and adequate warmth are essential, as are a constant supply of fresh, cool water, and foods to tempt the appetite.

Special equipment is not ordinarily needed, but the following items will be useful in caring for a sick dog, as well as in giving first aid for injuries:

petroleum jelly	tincture of metaphen
rubbing alcohol	cotton, gauze, and adhesive tape
mineral oil	burn ointment
rectal thermometer	tweezers
hydrogen peroxide	boric acid solution (2%)

If special medication is prescribed, it may be administered in any one of several ways. A pill or small capsule may be concealed in a small piece of meat, which the dog will usually swallow with no problem. A large capsule may be given by holding the dog's mouth open, inserting the capsule as far as possible down the throat, then holding the mouth closed until the dog swallows. Liquid medicine should be measured into a small bottle or test tube. Then, if the corner of the dog's lip is pulled out while the head is tilted upward, the liquid can be poured between the lips and teeth, a small amount at a time. If he refuses to swallow, keeping the dog's head tilted and stroking his throat will usually induce swallowing.

Foods offered the sick dog should be particularly nutritious and easily digested. Meals should be smaller than usual and offered at more frequent intervals. If the dog is reluctant to eat, offer food he particularly likes and warm it slightly to increase aroma and thus make it more tempting.

Housing Your Dog

Every dog should have a bed of his own, snug and warm, where he can retire undisturbed when he wishes to nap. And, especially with a small puppy, it is desirable to have the bed arranged so the dog can be securely confined at times, safe and contented. If the puppy is taught early in life to stay quietly in his box at night, or when the family is out, the habit will carry over into adulthood and will benefit both dog and master.

The dog should never be banished to a damp, cold basement, but should be quartered in an out-of-the-way corner close to the center of family activity. His bed can be an elaborate cushioned affair with electric warming pad, or simply a rectangular wooden box or heavy paper carton, cushioned with a clean cotton rug or towel. Actually, the latter is ideal for a new puppy, for it is snug, easy to clean, and expendable. A "door" can be cut on one side of the box for easy access, but it should be placed in such a way that the dog can still be confined when desirable.

The shipping crates used by professional handlers at dog shows make ideal indoor quarters. They are lightweight but strong, provide adequate air circulation, yet are snug and warm and easily cleaned. For the dog owner who takes his dog along when he travels, a dog crate is ideal, for the dog will willingly stay in his accustomed bed during long automobile trips, and the crate can be taken inside motels or hotels at night, making the dog a far more acceptable guest.

Dog crates are made of chromed metal or wood, and some have tops covered with a special rubber matting so they can be used as grooming tables. Anyone moderately handy with tools can construct a crate similar to the one illustrated on page 35.

Crates come in various sizes, to suit various breeds of dogs. For reasons of economy, the size selected for a puppy should be adequate for use when the dog is full grown. If the area seems too large when the puppy is small, a temporary cardboard partition can be installed to limit the area he occupies.

The dog owner who lives in the suburbs or in the country may want to keep a mature dog outdoors part of the time, in which case an outdoor doghouse should be provided. This type of kennel can also be constructed by the home handyman, but must be more substantial than quarters used indoors.

Outside finish of the doghouse can be of any type, but double wall construction will make for greater warmth in chilly weather. The floor should be smooth and easy to clean, so tongued and grooved boards or plywood are best. To keep the floor from contact with the damp earth, supports should be laid flat on the ground, running lengthwise of the structure. 2 x 4s serve well as supports for doghouses for small or medium breeds, but 4 x 4s should be used for large breeds.

The outdoor kennel must be big enough so that the dog can turn around inside, but small enough so that his body heat will keep it warm in chilly weather. The overall length of the kennel shoud be twice the length of the adult dog, measured from tip of nose to onset of tail. Width of the structure should be approximately three-fourths the length. And height from the floor to the point where the roof begins should be approximately one and a half the adult dog's height at the shoulders. If you build the house when the dog is still a puppy, you can determine his approximate adult size by referring to the Standard for his breed.

An "A" type roof is preferable, and an overhang of six inches all the way around will provide protection from sun and rain. If the roof is hinged to fold back, the interior of the kennel can be cleaned readily.

The entrance should be placed to one side rather than in the center, which will provide further protection against the weather. One of the commercially made door closures of rubber will keep out rain, snow, and wind, yet give the pet complete freedom to enter and leave his home.

The best location for the doghouse is where it will get enough morning sun to keep it dry, yet will not be in full sun during hot afternoons. If possible, the back of the doghouse should be placed toward the prevailing winds.

A fenced run or yard is essential to the outdoor kennel, and the fence must be sturdy enough that the dog cannot break through it, and high enough so he cannot jump or climb over it. The gate should have a latch of a type that can't be opened accidentally. The area enclosed must provide the dog with space to exercise freely, or else the dog must be exercised on the leash every day, for no dog should be confined to a tiny yard day after day without adequate exercise.

The yard must be kept clean and odor free, and the doghouse must be scrubbed and disinfected at frequent intervals. One of the insecticides made especially for use in kennels—one with a four to six weeks' residual effect—should be used regularly on floors and walls, inside and out.

Enough bedding must be provided so the dog can snuggle into it and keep warm in chilly weather. Bedding should either be of a type that is inexpensive, so it can be discarded and replaced frequently, or of a type that can be laundered readily. Dogs are often allergic to fungi found on straw, hay, or grass, and sometimes newspaper ink, but cedar shavings and old cotton rugs and blankets usually serve very well.

The Stone-age Dog

A Spotted Dog from India, "Parent of the Modern Coach dog."

History of
the Genus Canis

The history of man's association with the dog is a fascinating one, extending into the past at least seventy centuries, and involving the entire history of civilized man from the early Stone Age to the present.

The dog, technically a member of the genus *Canis,* belongs to the zoological family group *Canidae,* which also includes such animals as wolves, foxes, jackals, and coyotes. In the past it was generally agreed that the dog resulted from the crossing of various members of the family *Canidae.* Recent findings have amended this theory somewhat, and most authorities now feel the jackal probably has no direct relationship with the dog. Some believe dogs are descended from wolves and foxes, with the wolf the main progenitor. As evidence, they cite the fact that the teeth of the wolf are identical in every detail with those of the dog, whereas the teeth of the jackal are totally different.

Still other authorities insist that the dog always has existed as a separate and distinct animal. This group admits that it is possible for a dog to mate with a fox, coyote, or wolf, but points out that the resulting puppies are unable to breed with each other, although they can breed with stock of the same genus as either parent. Therefore, they insist, it was impossible for a new and distinct genus to have developed from such crossings. They then cite the fact that any dog can be mated with any other dog and the progeny bred among themselves. These researchers point out, too, heritable characteristics that are totally different in the three animals. For instance, the pupil of the dog's eye is round, that of the wolf oblique, and that of the jackal vertical. Tails, too, differ considerably, for tails of foxes, coyotes, and wolves always drop behind them, while those of dogs may be carried over the back or straight up.

Much conjecture centers on two wild dog species that still exist—the Dingo of Australia, and the Dhole in India. Similar in appearance, both are reddish in color, both have rather long, slender jaws, both have rounded ears that stand straight up, and both species hunt in packs. Evidence indicates that they had the same ancestors. Yet, today, they live in areas that are more than 4,000 miles apart.

Despite the fact that it is impossible to determine just when the dog first appeared as a distinct species, archeologists have found definite proof that the dog was the first animal domesticated by man. When man lived by tracking, trapping, and killing game, the dog added to the forces through which man discovered and captured the quarry. Man shared his primitive living quarters with the dog, and the two together devoured the prey. Thus, each helped to sustain the life of the other. The dog assisted man, too, by defending the campsite against marauders. As man gradually became civilized, the dog's usefulness was extended to guarding the other animals man domesticated, and, even before the wheel was invented, the dog served as a beast of burden. In fact, archeological findings show that aboriginal peoples of Switzerland and Ireland used the dog for such purposes long before they learned to till the soil.

Cave drawings from the palaeolithic era, which was the earliest part of the Old World Stone Age, include hunting scenes in which a rough, canine-like form is shown alongside huntsmen. One of these drawings is believed to be 50,000 years old, and gives credence to the theory that all dogs are descended from a primitive type ancestor that was neither fox nor wolf.

Archeological findings show that Europeans of the New Stone Age possessed a breed of dogs of wolf-like appearance, and a similar breed has been traced through the successive Bronze Age and Iron Age. Accurate details are not available, though, as to the external appearance of domesticated dogs prior to historic times (roughly four to five thousand years ago).

Early records in Chaldean and Egyptian tombs show that several distinct and well-established dog types had been developed by about 3700 B.C. Similar records show that the early people of the Nile Valley regarded the dog as a god, often burying it as a mummy in special cemeteries and mourning its death.

Some of the early Egyptian dogs had been given names, such as Akna, Tarn, and Abu, and slender dogs of the Greyhound type and a short-legged Terrier type are depicted in drawings found

Bas-relief of Hunters with Nets and Mastiffs. From the walls of Assurbanipal's palace at Nineveh 668-626 B.C. *British Museum.*

in Egyptian royal tombs that are at least 5,000 years old. The Afghan Hound and the Saluki are shown in drawings of only slightly later times. Another type of ancient Egyptian dog was much heavier and more powerful, with short coat and massive head. These probably hunted by scent, as did still another type of Egyptian dog that had a thick furry coat, a tail curled almost flat over the back, and erect "prick" ears.

Early Romans and Greeks mentioned their dogs often in literature, and both made distinctions between those that hunted by sight and those that hunted by scent. The Romans' canine classifications were similar to those we use now. In addition to dogs comparable to the Greek sight and scent hounds, the ancient Romans had Canes *villatici* (housedogs) and Canes *pastorales* (sheepdogs), corresponding to our present-day working dogs.

The dog is mentioned many times in the Old Testament. The first reference, in Genesis, leads some Biblical scholars to assert that man and dog have been companions from the time man was created. And later Biblical references bring an awareness of the diversity in breeds and types existing thousands of years ago.

As civilization advanced, man found new uses for dogs. Some required great size and strength. Others needed less of these characteristics but greater agility and better sight. Still others needed an accentuated sense of smell. As time went on, men kept those puppies that suited specific purposes especially well and bred them together. Through ensuing generations of selective breeding, desirable characteristics appeared with increasing frequency. Dogs used in a particular region for a special purpose gradually became more like each other, yet less like dogs of other areas used for different purposes. Thus were established the foundations for the various breeds we have today.

The American Kennel Club, the leading dog organization in the United States, divides the various breeds into six "Groups," based on similarity of purposes for which they were developed.

"Sporting Dogs" include the Pointers, Setters, Spaniels, and Retrievers that were developed by sportsmen interested in hunting game birds. Most of the Pointers and Setters are of comparatively recent origin. Their development parallels the development of sporting firearms, and most of them evolved in the British Isles. Exceptions are the Weimaraner, which was developed in Germany, and the Vizsla, or Hungarian Pointer, believed to have been developed by the Magyar hordes that swarmed over Central Europe a thousand years ago. The Irish were among the first to use Spaniels, though the name indicates that the original stock may have come from Spain. Two Sporting breeds, the American Water Spaniel, and the Chesapeake Bay Retriever, were developed entirely in the United States.

"Hounds," among which are Dachshunds, Beagles, Bassets, Harriers, and Foxhounds, are used singly, in pairs, or in packs to "course" (or run) and hunt for rabbits, foxes, and various rodents. But little larger, the Norwegian Elkhound is used in its native country to hunt big game—moose, bear, and deer.

The smaller Hound breeds hunt by scent, while the Irish Wolfhound, Borzoi, Scottish Deerhound, Saluki, and Greyhound hunt by sight. The Whippet, Saluki, and Greyhound are notably fleet of foot, and racing these breeds (particularly the Greyhound) is popular sport.

The Bloodhound is a member of the Hound Group that is known world-wide for its scenting ability. On the other hand, the Basenji is a comparatively rare Hound breed and has the distinction of being the only dog that cannot bark.

"Working Dogs" have the greatest utilitarian value of all modern dogs and contribute to man's welfare in diverse ways. The Boxer, Doberman Pinscher, Rottweiler, German Shepherd, Great Dane, and Giant Schnauzer are often trained to serve as sentries and aid police in patrolling streets. The German Shepherd is especially noted as a guide dog for the blind. The Collie, the various breeds of Sheepdogs, and the two Corgi breeds are known throughout the world for their extraordinary herding ability. And the exploits of the St. Bernard and Newfoundland are legendary, their records for saving lives unsurpassed.

The Siberian Husky and the Alaskan Malamute are noted for tremendous strength and stamina. Had it not been for these hardy Northern breeds, the great polar expeditions might never have taken place, for Admiral Byrd used these dogs to reach points inaccessible by other means. Even today, with our jet-age transportation, the Northern breeds provide a more practical means of travel in frigid areas than do modern machines.

"Terriers" derive their name from the Latin *terra,* meaning

1. The Newfoundland. 2. The English Setter. 3. The Large Water-spaniel.
4. The Terrier. 5. The Cur-dog. 6. The Shepherd's Dog. 7. The Bulldog. 8. The
Mastiff. 9. The Greenland Dog. 10. The Rought Water-dog. 11. The Small
Water-spaniel. 12. The Old English Hound. 13. The Dalmatian or Coach-dog.
14. The Comporter (very much of a Papillon). 15. "Toy Dog, Bottle, Glass,
and Pipe." *From a vignette.* 16. The Springer or Cocker. *From Thomas
Bewick's "General History of Quadrupeds" (1790).*

"earth," for all of the breeds in this Group are fond of burrowing.
Terriers hunt by digging into the earth to rout rodents and fur-
bearing animals such as badgers, woodchucks, and otters. Some
breeds are expected merely to force the animals from their dens
in order that the hunter can complete the capture. Others are
expected to find and destroy the prey, either on the surface or
under the ground.

Terriers come in a wide variety of sizes, ranging from such large breeds as the Airedale and Kerry Blue to such small ones as the Skye, the Dandie Dinmont, the West Highland White, and the Scottish Terrier. England, Ireland, and Scotland produced most of the Terrier breeds, although the Miniature Schnauzer was developed in Germany.

"Toys," as the term indicates, are small breeds. Although they make little claim to usefulness other than as ideal housepets, Toy dogs develop as much protective instinct as do larger breeds and serve effectively in warning of the approach of strangers.

Origins of the Toys are varied. The Pekingese was developed as the royal dog of China more than two thousand years before the birth of Christ. The Chihuahua, smallest of the Toys, originated in Mexico and is believed to be a descendant of the Techichi, a dog of great religious significance to the Aztecs, while the Italian Greyhound was popular in the days of ancient Pompeii.

"Non-Sporting Dogs" include a number of popular breeds of varying ancestry. The Standard and Miniature Poodles were developed in France for the purpose of retrieving game from water. The Bulldog originated in Great Britain and was bred for the purpose of "baiting" bulls. The Chowchow apparently originated centuries ago in China, for it is pictured in a bas relief dated to the Han dynasty of about 150 B.C.

The Dalmatian served as a carriage dog in Dalmatia, protecting travelers in bandit-infested regions. The Keeshond, recognized as the national dog of Holland, is believed to have originated in the Arctic or possibly the Sub-Arctic. The Schipperke, sometimes erroneously described as a Dutch dog, originated in the Flemish provinces of Belgium. And the Lhasa Apso came from Tibet, where it is known as "Abso Seng Kye," the "Bark Lion Sentinel Dog."

During the thousands of years that man and dog have been closely associated, a strong affinity has been built up between the two. The dog has more than earned his way as a helper, and his faithful, selfless devotion to man is legendary. The ways in which the dog has proved his intelligence, his courage, and his dependability in situations of stress are amply recorded in the countless tales of canine heroism that highlight the pages of history, both past and present.

63

Dogs in Woodcuts. (*1st row*) (LEFT) "Maltese dog with shorter hair";
(RIGHT) "Spotted sporting dog trained to catch game"; (*2nd row*) (LEFT)
Sporting white dog; (RIGHT) "Spanish dog with floppy ears": (*3rd row*)
(LEFT) "French dog"; (RIGHT) "Mad dog of Grevinus"; (*4th row*) (LEFT)
Hairy Maltese dog; (RIGHT) "English fighting dog . . . of horrid aspect." *From
Aldrovandus (1637).*

History of the Maltese

Establishing the exact origins of a breed of dog that is very old is at best a most inexact science. Breeds that have been created in the last one hundred to two hundred years are relatively easy to trace because of the conscientious record-keeping on the part of the breeders. This is, however, not true of the ancient breeds that have gone through centuries of evolution.

Such is the case of the Maltese. The breed—or, more precisely, the type—has existed for hundreds of years. In both literature and art there is concrete evidence of the early existence of the Maltese.

The weight of the evidence seems to indicate that the island of Malta in the Mediterranean is the point of departure for tracing the origin of the Maltese. This is not to state that the breed is native to this small island, but rather to indicate that it was from here that interest in the breed has been disseminated in the most recent past.

The island of Malta is located in the middle of the Mediterranean Sea at the junction of the eastern and western basins. The island is extremely small, measuring only seventeen miles long and nine miles wide. The size, however, is not indicative of its importance. This tiny island is located 180 miles from Africa, 60 miles from Sicily, and 140 miles from Europe. There is geological evidence that during the Pleistocene Age the island was connected to Italy by a narrow neck of land which has since submerged. Traditions that started there when the island was part of the mainland would continue but would, of course, be modified by other forces with the passing of the centuries. It may be concluded, then, that if the Maltese-type dog were popular on the Continent, he would be popular on the island.

An island as small as Malta would not tolerate an invasion by a population of large animals. Those animals, with the exception of the goat, that were brought to the island throughout the centuries would have to have been on the small side. Conditions would permit only small house pets rather than the large guard dogs so popular with high officials through the years.

Ch. Bayhammond's Tomi Dancer, owned by Mrs. Bessie Crowe.

Am. & Can. Ch. Couer-De-Lion, owned by Mr. & Mrs. Ted. J. Dillon.

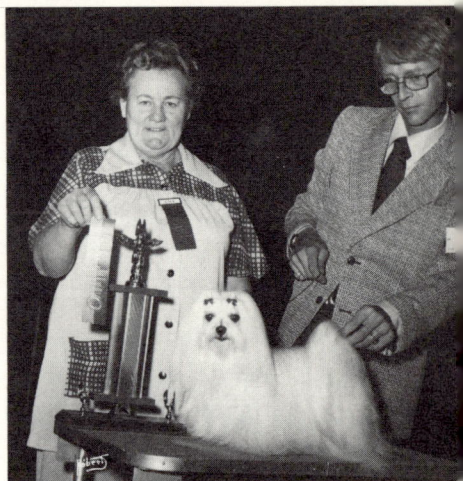

Ch. Martae Mona, owned by Mrs. Martha B. Davidson.

The strategic location of Malta has been evident from the beginning of the expansion of trade routes. The Phoenicians established colonies there in their move toward western expansion. These were taken over by the Carthaginians in the sixth century before the birth of Christ. Succeeding invasions were made by the Romans, the Turks, the Arabs, and the Normans. The island finally had a relatively long period of peace and stability starting in 1530, when it became the fiefdom of the Knights of St. John of Jerusalem. It remained under the British rule of the Knights until independence was granted in 1964. The population has grown from 21,000 during the time of the Norman invasion to approximately one-third of a million today.

Small lap dogs or ladies' dogs existed in many parts of the world at the time of the Phoenician and Carthaginian domination of the Mediterranean lands and were probably brought to the island by traders. Some of these dogs were brought from Roman Egypt at the time of the birth of Christ.

Certain *objets d'art*, such as vases and stone carvings of the Egyptians, the Greeks, and the Romans of this period, give evidence of the existence of such small, moderately coated little dogs, which appear to be solid-colored and light in pigmentation. While these small dogs may originally have had a working function such as that of the burrower or the ratter, it seems evident that by this time they were more of a status symbol than anything else.

There is also evidence in literature that such dogs did in fact exist. It has been established that the Emperor Claudius had such a dog, and references are made to the breed by Aristotle and Pliny as well. It seems only natural that if this little dog was a status symbol among the ruling class of Rome, he would also have the same importance in the colonies. This is evidenced by the fact that Publius, the Roman governor of Malta, had a small house dog pet of the Maltese type that he called Issa, after the island. To retain its prestige, the breed was carefully guarded and ownership was limited to the elite.

During the centuries, the dog has been called by a series of names: the Maltese, the Melita, the Melitei, and the Bichon. The latter name seems to lend strength to the contention of those who believe that the Bichon Frise and the Maltese are really only different strains of the same breed. Little real confusion exists among the first three names when it is remembered that Melita was the Carthaginian name for the island and that Melitei is the genitive case of the Latin word and means "of Malta."

Ch. Cotterell's Rascals Tid Bit, owned by Agnes E. Cotterell.

Ch. Russ Ann Petite Charmer, owned by Anna Mae Hardy.

Ch. Su-Le's Love Bird, owned by Barbara J. Berquist.

There was early confusion in classifying the Maltese as either a Spaniel or a Terrier. Bone structure analysis, especially that of the head, gives strong support to the belief that the dog belongs to the Spaniel family.

The title "Lion Dog" is used occasionally to refer to the Maltese. This has given rise to the discussion that the dog is perhaps of Oriental origin and belongs to the same family as the Lhasa Apso, the Pekingese, and the Shih Tzu. There is more than superficial evidence for such a belief. As overland trade routes were opened to the Orient and East-West trade was established on a regular basis, the possibility of such a point of origin for the Maltese could exist.

This, in reality, does not seem to be the case. Again a skeletal examination of the four breeds indicates basic differences in rib structure, shoulder placement, and especially angulation which would affect rear movement. The most conclusive piece of evidence against an Oriental origin is undoubtedly the coat of the Maltese. It is a single coat having no undercoat. This is an indication that the Maltese is a breed originating in a warm climate such as the Mediterranean area has, and not from a colder climate such as that of Tibet or China.

The truth of the matter probably is that the Maltese traveled from West to East rather than from East to West. In an effort to ingratiate himself with the men of influence in the Orient, the trader carried little dogs as gifts. This was in keeping with long-established tradition in China and Tibet, for the emperors of China and Dalai Lamas of Tibet exchanged Pekingese and Lhasa Apsos on special occasions. The Shih Tzu is the result of such customs, for he is the result of a cross between the Pekingese and the Lhasa Apso.

The Maltese was undoubtedly used in a similar fashion; and because of a lack of the purist rules of breeding that exist today, he was probably cross-bred with all three Oriental breeds. This would explain the recessive white gene that is carried in these Oriental breeds today.

During those early centuries of its existence in the Mediterranean, the little Maltese-type dog of Egypt was undoubtedly crossed to the Spitz-type dog of central Europe. This would have modified size, but would also have increased stamina and bone. This Spitz-Pomeranian type cross was common in other Toy breeds for a period of time.

Crossing of breeds would, of course, result in a two-way exchange of influences. Not only was the color of the Maltese transmitted to the Oriental breeds and possibly to the Spitz-Pomeranian type, but certainly their color was transmitted to the Maltese. These crosses can explain the presence of tan or the lemon color on the early white Maltese, and the existence of the colored Maltese seen in Europe at the beginning of the century.

The Maltese had an advantage that these other breeds did not enjoy. It was the factor of a controlled breeding situation. Crosses were for the most part intentional rather than casual or accidental. With the complete isolation of the island of Malta, the Maltese tended to be inbred constantly, which, over a period of time, would dilute non-typical breed factors. This same set of circumstances would not exist, of course, for the other breeds. Consistency of type would seem to give strong support to the belief that the Maltese, while perhaps not native to the island of Malta, was purified there.

The island of Malta influenced the popularity of the Maltese in modern times as well. The Knights of St. John of Jerusalem were an order of British origin. Their control and domination of the island for a period of several centuries was felt in England itself. England at this time was one of the world's great sea powers, and the island of Malta served as a haven and way station for the ships that operated the trade routes of the Mediterranean and the Middle East.

It was a strong British tradition that customs that existed in England existed in her colonies and that the good that existed in the colonies was to be brought back to the mother country. This was also the case with the Maltese dog. Beginning in the 1500s, specimens of the breed were brought back to the court of England. While there was a certain novelty in the little Toy dogs, they did not gain great popularity. They were really not suited to living conditions that existed in the England of the Renaissance. The climate was much too severe for the tiny dogs bred in a very warm climate, and the total lack of central heating would have been intolerable for them. Furthermore, the taste of the English at this time ran more toward large hunting dogs and guard dogs.

By the eighteenth century both living conditions and the national personality of England and the Continent as a whole were changing. The Maltese were again imported in very limited numbers and this time received a limited but more cordial reception. It was not, however, until Queen Victoria received a Maltese as a gift that the breed became generally accepted. It is interesting to note that the

Ch. Joanne-Chen's
Maja Dancer,
owned by Jo Ann
Dinsmore.

dog given to the Queen did not come directly from Malta but rather was brought from Manila by one of the ships of the Royal Navy. The fact that this dog came from the Orient is further evidence of the interchange of gifts of dogs between the West and East. Several of the breeds that exist in England today are there because early specimens were brought back by returning sailors.

The royal favor changed the national tastes, resulting in the acceptance of the Maltese as a breed recognized by the English Kennel Club. In 1859 a Maltese dog named Psyche was finally entered in a match in England.

Ch. Baldino of Villa
Malta, owned by
the Author.

Ch. Cotterell's Kippi Kai O Rascal, owned by Mrs. June Nay.

Am. & Can. Ch. Patrick Al-Mar of Villa Malta (left) and Am. & Can. Ch. Wif 'n' Poof Al-Mar of Villa Malta were owned by Marjorie Lewis.

The Maltese in the United States, 1888-1960

While specimens of Maltese were arriving in the United States in limited numbers during the early nineteenth century, it was not until 1888 that The American Kennel Club officially opened the studbook for Maltese. Only two bitches were registered in that year, both of unknown pedigree. They were Snips and Topsy, the latter being an import.

The next entries in the studbook were not made until 1901, when two more bitches were entered, one being an import. In 1902 four dogs and two bitches were registered. Registrations increased and by the 1950s they had passed the fifty mark.

Maltese were originally entered in shows in the Miscellaneous Class and then were transferred to the Non-Sporting Group before finally being assigned to the Toy Group.

One of the first Maltese kennels established in the United States was Thackery Kennel of Mrs. C. S. Young of New York. Her Thackery Rob Roy (whelped 1901) was the first champion and his name was recorded in the studbook in 1904. He was bred to Thackery Lady Kathleen and from this litter came Thackery Bonnie Lassie (1904), whose name can be seen in many of the early Maltese Pedigrees.

Rossmore Kennel of Mrs. Gertrude Phalen of Illinois was operating about the same time as was Thackery Kennel. One of the first breedings at Rossmore produced Ch. Baby Boy (1901). A repeat breeding in 1902 produced Ch. Tiny Boy. Ch. Baby Boy proved his worth as a sire in his famous son Ch. Sonny Boy (1902).

Mrs. Carl Baumann of Brooklyn, New York, established Dyker Kennel before World War I and continued breeding until after the war. Her Ch. Dyker Dolly II (1911) attracted great interest in the breed at dog shows in the area. Dolly's son Ch. Sweetsir of Dyker (1912) had the great honor of winning a Best-in-Show award. Two additional champions were bred in 1915—Ch. Dyker Snowshell of Esperance and Ch. Dyker Major Mite. Ch. Lady Dolly of Dyker (1919) was popular in the show ring in the early 1920s.

Mrs. Anna Judd of Seattle, Washington, opened her Melita Kennel shortly before World War I. Her Melita Cupid (1914) had the distinction of becoming an International Champion. Other winners of note from this kennel were Ch. Melita Snow Dream (1915), Ch. Melita Prince Lilywhite (1918), and Ch. Queen of Melita (1919).

Mrs. Agnes Rossman of New York brought interest to her Arr Kennel with her first champion, Lady Anna of Arr (1916). The practice of using royal titles was continued with Ch. Lady Issa of Arr (1918), Ch. Sir Lars of Arr (1918), Ch. Lady Clio of Arr (1921), and Ch. Sir Irak of Arr (1921).

Hale Farm Kennel of Beverly, Massachusetts, was one of the truly great Maltese kennels of all times. For her original stock, Miss Eleanor Bancroft went to both Dyker and Arr Kennels. Dogs of these breedings figure prominently in all Hale Farm pedigrees. Ch. Sheila of Hale Farm (1927) was the dam of two fine producers: Ch Circe of Hale Farm (1929) and Ch. Bob Snow White of Hale Farm (1929). Circe was the dam of the great stud dog Ch. Cupid of Hale Farm (1935).

Dr. Vincenzo Calvaresi bought several Maltese from Hale Farm when that kennel disbanded its breeding program. These dogs served as foundation stock for the world-famous Villa Malta Kennel located in Bedford, Massachusetts. Dr. Calvaresi started his breeding program in the late 1930s and continued it up until the mid-1960s when he retired and moved to Florida. Villa Malta Kennel has the distinction of being the first kennel in the United States to have finished over one hundred champions. This record has since been broken in other breeds but it stood alone for several years.

In addition to his Hale Farm stock, Dr. Calvaresi was able to purchase several fine show specimens from Mrs. Nadya Colombo of Milan, Italy. Mrs. Colombo shipped the dogs from her Electa Kennel shortly after World War II. These dogs were outstanding in head, and in both quantity and texture of coat. They passed these qualities on to the Villa Malta line. Three of these outstanding champions, all sired by Italian Ch. Electa Eolo but each out of a different dam, are: Ch. Electa Brio, Ch. Electa Pampi, and Ch. Electa Laila.

Ch. Vivia of Villa Malta (1940) was the first to carry the kennel name to championship. She was the dam of several winners and started a long uninterrupted line of champions. Her son Ch. Gitano of Villa Malta sired Ch. Nino of Villa Malta, who sired Ch. Tristan of Villa Malta, the sire of five champions. One of Tristan's sons was the all-time great sire, Ch. Ricco of Villa Malta, the sire of forty-one champions. Ricco was the sire of Ch. Patrick Al-Mar of Villa Malta, the top producing stud of Marjorie Lewis's Al-Mar Kennel in Independence, Missouri. Ch. Musi of Villa Malta, another son of Ricco, was the sire of fifteen champions. Musi's son, American and Canadian Ch. Tico of Villa Malta, went to the Good Time Kennel of Mr. and Mrs. Robert Craig and figures prominently in Good Time pedigrees.

Dr. Calvaresi has left his mark on Maltese history not only because of his breeding program, but also because of his great showmanship. He focused national interest on the Maltese in the 1940s and 1950s with the braces and teams that he exhibited at shows across the country. The perfectly matched teams of champions were precision trained and consequently were able to capture numerous Best-in-Show awards. Not only did dedicated breeders come to Villa Malta Kennel to purchase their breeding stock, but also many celebrities who were seeking a prestige pet.

The last of the kennels of the early and middle years to be included in this chapter is Jon Vir Kennel located in Riverdale, Maryland. Mrs. Virginia T. Leitch not only purchased the foundation stock from Villa Malta Kennel, but also imported breeding stock. She was especially interested in the English dogs from Harlingen Kennel and those from Suirside Kennel located in Ireland. While Mrs. Leitch did not show as extensively as some of the other kennel owners, she did continue a very active breeding program. Her Ch. Jon Vir's Tiny Boy was the sire of Ch. Jon Vir's First Lady and Ch. Jon Vir's Smart Trick. Other winners carrying the kennel prefix are Ch. Jon Vir's Dusty Cavalier and Ch. Jon Vir's Minuet.

Even if Mrs. Leitch had not established a fine record as both a breeder and an exhibitor, she would still have been highly regarded by all dedicated Maltese breeders. It was Mrs. Leitch who, in 1953, published an exhaustive history of the breed, *The Maltese Dog*. This book offered valuable information and many photographs of the Maltese, and it was so immensely popular that all copies were sold after a very brief period of time.

Ch. Russ Ann Honey of Marcris, owned by Anna Mae Hardy.

Ch. Trina of Primrose Place, owned by Marge Stuber.

Ch. Aennchen's Paris Dancer, owned by Dr. & Mrs. Kenneth Knopf.

Ch. Aennchen's Suni Dancer, owned by Dr. & Mrs. Roger T. Brown.

Ch. Aennchen's Taja Dancer, owned by Mrs. J. P. Antonelli.

Am., Can., & Ber. Ch. Nyssamead's Dhugal, owned by Mrs. Claudette LeMay.

The Maltese in the United States Since 1960

There are many kennels that have been breeding and showing Maltese for the past ten or fifteen years, and still others that were active for a year or two and then discontinued their breeding and showing programs. To offer a picture of the present day Maltese, a limited number of representative kennels from throughout the country have been selected. These kennels have not only made significant contributions in improving the quality of the breed, but also stimulated interest in the breed, thus increasing its overall popularity.

The kennels presented here are in alphabetical order according to kennel prefix.

It would be appropriate, even if an alphabetical listing were not considered, to start with Aennchen's Kennel of Mr. and Mrs. J. P. Antonelli. As the 1950s were dominated by Villa Malta Maltese, the 1960s have been most justifiably dominated by the Aennchen Maltese.

Aennchen Antonelli established her kennel in Waldwick, New Jersey, in the late 1950s. Maintaining a breeding program limited in quantity, but limitless in quality, the Antonellis have bred many champions. Their American and Bermudian Ch. Aennchen's Raja Yoga was the sire of nineteen champions and was the top Maltese sire in 1961. Raja was a grandson of the great Ch. Electa Pampi and International Ch. Electa Laila. His daughter Ch. Aennchen's Puja Dancer was herself the dam of seven champions and won the top honors for Maltese dams in 1961.

The list of the champions carrying the Aennchen affix is so long that it is difficult to select a limited few. One of the outstanding ones was Ch. Aennchen's Shikar Dancer, co-owned with Mrs. Joanne Hesse. He was not only a great showman, but also a great sire. His daughter Ch. Co-Ca-He's Aennchen Toy Dancer, owned by Miss Anne Marie Stimmler, was a multiple Best-in-Show winner and went Best of Breed at the first Maltese Specialty, which was held in 1966. Ch. Aennchen's Poona Dancer, co-owned by Frank Oberstar and Larry Ward, won thirty-eight Best-in-Show awards, a

Ch. Joanne-Chen's Maya
Dancer, owned by Mrs.
Mamie Gregory.

Ch. March'en Martini Dancer,
owned by Marcia Hostetler.

Ch. Spring Holly's Passin'
Fancy, owned by Delores
Lewis and Maurine
Middleton.

breed record which went unbroken for several years. Poona won the Maltese Specialty in 1967. Other Best-in-Show winners are Ch. Aennchen's Taja Dancer, owned by the Antonellis, and Ch. Aennchen's Paris Dancer, owned by Dr. and Mrs. Kenneth Knopf. The names of other Aennchen dogs can be found in the pedigrees of other leading show winners which do not carry the kennel name.

Aga Lynn Kennel, located in Glen Cove, New York, is a small kennel but still has produced a number of champions. Among them are Ch. Aga Lynn Dancing Raja, Ch. Aga Lynn Boona Cheema, Ch. Aga Lynn Doodle Dancer, and Ch. Aga Lynn Sassy Girl.

Dorothy Tinker operates Al-Dor Kennel in Las Vegas, Nevada. Winners carrying the kennel prefix are Ch. Al-Dor Little Fella of Vegas, Ch. Al-Dor Nicy of Vegas, Ch. Al-Dor Little Rascal, and Ch. Al-Dor Pzazz. Pzazz was specialed for owners Art and Grace Hendrickson of Los Angeles.

Al-Mar Kennel of Mrs. Marjorie Lewis is located in Independence, Missouri. An all-breed professional handler for many years, Mrs. Lewis has finished more than fifty Maltese champions under her Al-Mar Kennel prefix. In addition to Maltese, she also breeds and has finished champion Lhasa Apsos and champion Shih Tzus.

Al-Mar's top producing home-bred, Ch. Patrick Al-Mar of Villa Malta, was the sire of many champions. Other winners from this kennel are Ch. Tiny Tanella of Al-Mar, Ch. Tiny Scooter of Al-Mar, Ch. Little Dark Eyes of Al-Mar, and Ch. Isabella of Al-Mar. Al-Mar Maltese have been known by their diminutive size and their soundness.

Alice Pond's Alpond Kennel is located in Ohio. Ch. Alpond's Sky Rockette, owned by Mrs. Frances Geraghty, finished her title at ten months of age by going Best of Winners at the 1966 Maltese Specialty. Other winners are Ch. Alpond's Shine Little Star, Ch. Alpond's Scamperino, and Ch. Alpond's Star Baby.

Bayhammond's Kennel, located in the Midwest, has bred several champions. Bayhammond's dogs can be recognized by their beautiful coats. Winners include Ch. Bayhammond's Triplet Dancer, Ch. Bayhammond's Tomi Dancer, Ch. Bayhammond's Tina Dancer, and Ch. Bayhammond's Dancer's Image.

The West Coast offers Bejune Kennel, located in Santa Rosa, California. Representative types from this kennel include Ch. Bejune's Top O the Mark, Ch. Bejune's Mark Pompaduke Too, Ch. Bejune's Englander Tipster, and Ch. Bejune's Maxim of Llonnee Lane.

More than two dozen champions carry the banner of Bobbelee Kennel, owned by Mrs. Roberta Harrison and located in Miami, Florida. Ch. Bobbelee Hanky Panky, a Best-in-Show winner, has built a fine record in the ring as well as an outstanding record as a stud dog. Other typical winners from this kennel are: Ch. Bobbelee Marshmallow, Ch. Bobbelee Meringue, Ch. Bobbelee Constant Comment, and Ch. Bobbelee Brag-A-Bout. In addition to home-breds, Mrs. Harrison also owns the fine English import Ch. Leckhampton Sprig, a good representative of the breed in the show ring before he was retired to be a stud dog.

Patricia Howell established her Boreas Kennel in Hugo, Minnesota. In addition to breeding Maltese, Mrs. Howell is the author of *The Modern Maltese*. This book offers sound advice to both beginning and experienced breeders. Expertise to write this book was gained through the experience of operating a kennel that produced such winners as Ch. Boreas Rex, Ch. Boreas Rex Delphinium, and Ch. Boreas Don't Tread on Me. Ch. Boreas Bonitatis went Best in Show the first time out after being exported to Australia.

C and M Kennel based its breeding program on Villa Malta stock. A representative example of this type breeding is Ch. C and M's Camero of Villa Malta. Other titled dogs include Ch. C and M's Tiny Moonglow, Ch. C and M's Noble Faith, and Ch. C and M's Serina of Milottie.

Cla-Mal Kennel, owned by Mrs. Boyd Clark of Peel, Arkansas, finished several champions. Cla-Mal's showing program, however, was not as extensive as its breeding program and a number of fine but untitled Cla-Mal dogs can be found in current pedigrees. Show winners include Ch. Cla-Mal Angel of Miss Liberty, Ch. Cla-Mal Precious Arissa, Ch. Cla-Mal Fallow, and Ch. Cla-Mal Sir Jumbie.

The Northwest offers the Cotterell's Kennel of Agnes Cotterell, located in Boise, Idaho. In spite of the scarcity of dog shows in this part of the country, a number of championships have been completed. Among the winners are such dogs as Ch. Cotterell's Rascals Tid Bit, Ch. Cotterell's Luv of Tennessa, and Ch. Cotterell's Toppers Frosty.

Arlene Grady established her D'Arlene Kennel in the East. Her winners included Ch. D'Arlene's Meringue, Ch. D'Arlene's Tampico, Ch. D'Arlene's Kiu Kiu, and Ch. D'Arlene's Sol Hol.

Duncan Kennel of Fran Duncan, in Norfolk, Virginia, offers several dogs carrying the kennel prefix. Examples are Ch. Duncan's

Christopher, Ch. Duncan's Bagpipe, and Ch. Duncan's Nicholas. Nicholas has the honor of being a Best-in-Show winner. The stud dog Ch. Duncan's Kimberly has left his mark on a number of winning get.

More than a dozen champions carry the title from the Eckes Kennel. Among these winning Maltese are Ch. Eckes' Patty Patou, Ch. Eckes' Always on Sundays, Ch. Eckes' Top Hat in Tails, and Ch. Eckes' Good as Gold.

The Eve-Ron Kennel has followed a limited breeding and showing program. This philosophy has resulted in such winners as Ch. Eve-Ron's Tiffonie Doll, Ch. Eve-Ron's Tiny Topper, Ch. Eve-Ron's Snow Topper, and Ch. Eve-Ron's Snokist Cherub.

Faience Kennel of Russel Jackson in Collegeville, Pennsylvania, is another small operation. A limited breeding program has produced Ch. Faience Nickolo and Ch. Faience Jim-Jim.

Elvera Cox of Union City, Michigan, is the owner of Fairy Fay Kennel. The beautiful expressions she has bred into her line can be seen in Ch. Fairy Fay's Giorgi, Ch. Fairy Fay's Kapu, Ch. Fairy Fay's Peter Pan, and Ch. Fairy Fay's Minnissa. Fairy Fay's Figaro was sold to Dorothy Tinker of Al-Dor Kennel. He was campaigned and earned both his American and his Bermudian championships.

Harriet Taylor of California owns Folklore Kennel. An impressive winner in the late 1960s was Ch. Enricco, co-owned by Harriet Taylor and Lenard Reppond. Enricco became the top male Maltese in the United States in 1966 while he was still a puppy. Ch. Folklore True Blue is an example of the type that carries this prefix.

Gaybrick Kennel in Kansas is operated by Rita Brickley. Mrs. Brickley, an American Kennel Club judge, has bred both champion Cairns and champion Maltese. Her Ch. Gaybrick Little Rascal proved to be an outstanding stud dog. Other winners include Ch. Gaybrick Snow Crystal, Ch. Gaybrick Sugar of Fefes, and Ch. Snow Mittens of Gaybrick.

Robert and Eloise Craig of Normal, Illinois, have been dedicated Maltese breeders for more than a quarter of a century. Their Good Time Kennel is responsible for many champions and has been a source of breeding stock for many young kennels. Mrs. Craig served as a driving force in the establishment of the American Maltese Association and has been an officer in that organization since its founding. Also, she has been the Maltese columnist for the A.K.C. Gazette for years. Among the many winners from Good

Ch. Cuddledon's Maya Doll Prince, owned by Dr. & Mrs. Nelson King.

Ch. Pen Sans Moonshine, owned by Cecelia Olive.

Ch. Susie Sunflower of Al-Mar, owned by Marjorie Lewis.

Time are Ch. Good Time Prince Sunny Jim, Ch. Good Time Hilda, Ch. Good Time Gentleman Jim, and Ch. Good Time Chatterbox Lynn.

Gwenbrook Kennel, owned by Dr. and Mrs. Edwin Holbrook of Glen Head, New York, has operated on a small scale but has produced such stars as Ch. Gwenbrook Modesty and Ch. Gwenbrook Elena.

Another small kennel is Jambon Kennel, which finished Ch. Jambon Tiny Tim and Ch. Jambon Molly Malone.

Joanne Hesse started breeding Maltese with Aennchen Antonelli. Her first champions carried one prefix while later ones carried a modified version. Early champions were Ch. Jo-Aennchen Raja Dancer and Ch. Jo-Aennchen Dancing Dark Eyes. Mrs. Hesse's kennel, located in Indiana, now operates under the name of Joanne-Chen. Dozens of champions now carry this name. The current big winner has been Ch. Joanne-Chen's Maya Dancer, who is owned by Mrs. Mamie Gregory of Fort Lauderdale, Florida, and has been handled by Mrs. Peggy Hogg to a record breaking forty-three Best-in-Show awards. Ch. Joanne-Chen's Shikar Dancer and Ch. Joanne-Chen's Sweet He Dancer have been sold to Japan. Some others are Ch. Joanne-Chen's Siva Dancer, Ch. Joanne-Chen's Magi Dancer, Ch. Joanne-Chen's Square Dancer, and Ch. Joanne-Chen's Sweet She Dancer.

La Moda Kennel of Salem, Oregon, brought three of its Maltese into the winner's circle. They are Ch. La Moda's Lady in White, Ch. La Moda's White Simone, and Ch. La. Moda's White Johanne.

Lonesome Lane Kennel, in Midwest competition, finished Ch. Lauri of Lonesome Lane De Fefe and Ch. Lilly of Lonesome Lane.

Maltacello Kennel is located in Bethel Park, Pennsylvania, and is owned by Virginia Sunner Evans. Winners here include Ch. Angela Ka Doll of Maltacello, Ch. Sabrina of Maltacello, Ch. Maltacello Romeo, and Ch. Maltacello Feather Duster.

Mrs. Florence Hopple of Tiffin, Ohio, has a pair of dogs carrying her Malta Gables Kennel name. They are Ch. Hopple's Lisa of Malta Gables and Ch. L.G.D. Valentino of Malta Gables.

Rena Martin of Highland Park, Illinois, is a professional handler who started out breeding Maltese. In addition to the many champion Maltese she has finished, she has also bred Group winning Lhasa Apsos. Martin Maltese have won numerous Groups and several Best-in-Show awards. Winners from this kennel include

Ch. Martin Muffet Puff, Ch. Martin Jingles Puff, Ch. Martin Joker Puff, and Ch. Martin Doo Dad Puff.

Mrs. Martin's daughter Daryl showed Ch. Martin Flopsy Puff and Ch. Martin Candido as a brace while she was a junior handler and still in high school. This brace won many Groups and several Best-in-Show awards.

Michael Wolf calls his kennel Mike Mar. An owner of several breeds, he has achieved recognition in Maltese as well. Included among his winning Maltese are Ch. Mike Mar's Shikar's Replica, Ch. Mike Mar's Maji Puff, Ch. Mike Mar's Joanne-Chen's Dancer, Ch. Mike Mar's San-Su-Kee, and Ch. Mike Mar's My Twilight Dream.

Nyssamead Kennel is located in Connecticut and is owned by Susan M. Weber. Ch. Nyssamead's Dessa, Ch. Nyssamead's Chloe, and Ch. Nyssamead's Cicero are among the winners under this banner. Mrs. Claudette LeMay of Sugar Town Kennel has campaigned Nyssamead's Dhugal to his American, Canadian, and Bermudian championships.

Oak Hill finished several champions under its prefix. Among these are Ch. Oak Hill Dancer of Winddrift, Ch. Oak Hill Tedi Snow Crop, and Ch. Dwal's Violet of Oak Hill.

Mrs. Wilma Burg of Lumberville, Pennsylvania, owns Oak Manor Kennel. Among the more than forty champions owned by Mrs. Burg are Ch. Oak Manor Skylark, Ch. Oak Manor Skyliner, Ch. Oak Manor Enchantress, and Ch. Oak Manor Comet.

Anne Pendleton of Louisville, Ohio, has bred Yorkshire Terriers as well as Maltese. Under the Pendleton Kennel banner Mrs. Pendleton has had numerous Best-in-Show wins. An early winner was Ch. Brittigan's Sweet William. Ch. Pendleton's Peachytu became an American and Canadian champion and earned several Best-in-Show awards. Other winners are Ch. Pendleton's Boy's Boy, a Best-in-Show winner; Ch. Pendleton's Tar Baby; and Ch. Pendleton's Jewel. Jewel, owned by Dorothy White, was a multiple Best-in-Show winner under the capable handling of her owner.

Pen Sans Kennel is operated by Mrs. G. Busselman in Richland, Washington. A relatively new kennel, Pen Sans has established an enviable record. Ch. Pen Sans Moonshine has won a Best in Show for his owner, Cecelia Olive of Oklahoma. Other stars are: Ch. Pen Sans Magician, Ch. Pen Sans September Song, and Ch. Pen Sans Krista.

Mrs. Robert Stuber of Lima, Ohio, is the owner of Primrose Place Kennel. She is the author of the handbook *I Love Maltese*.

Mrs. Stuber's first brood bitch was an import from the Vicbrita Kennel in England. Her first home-bred was Ch. Robby of Primrose Place. He was followed by a line of champions that includes Ch. Trina of Primrose Place, Ch. Andrena of Primrose Place, Ch. Primrose Place Didi Roy of Sule, and Ch. Primrose Place Ursula Roy. Mrs. Stuber added the small showman Beland's Little Smarty to her kennel as a stud dog. He finished both his American and Canadian championships.

Among the champions that Jean Rand of North Miami, Florida, has finished are: Ch. Rand's Gorgeous George, Ch. Rand's White Magnolia, Ch. Rand's Top Hat of Shareen, and Ch. Rand's Stormy Weather Shareen.

Dr. Helen Schively Poggi of California was a most active sponsor in the founding of the American Maltese Association. Her Reveille Kennel is represented by Ch. Lester's Morning Reveille, Ch. Sir Soni Ravi Reveille, and Ch. Sonny Morning Reveille.

Mrs. Rose Anhell of Quincy, Illinois, added Maltese to her Ronell Kennel of Shetland Sheepdogs. Her Maltese winners include Ch. Ronell's White Starfire and Ch. Ronell's White Medallian. Mrs. Anhell also worked with her Maltese in obedience, and her Ronell's White Charmer earned his Companion Dog title.

Mrs. Ruth Roath purchased her foundation stud Starward's Comet from Starward Kennel in Ohio. Comet finished his championship and became the sire of Ch. Roath's Color Me Merry Too. Mrs. Roath purchased Stentaway's Drummer Boy, who has since become a champion in the United States, Canada, Mexico, and Bermuda. He also has the International CACIB.

Mrs. Anna Mae Hardy of Miami, Florida, owns Russ Ann Kennel. Two winners that carry the kennel prefix are Ch. Russ Ann Petite Charmer and Ch. Russ Ann Honey of Marcris.

Rustwick Kennel used double Electa breeding in establishing its kennel line. The Italian-bred Ch. Electa Eolo figures prominently in these pedigrees. An early winner, Ch. Rustwick Corina, was joined by Ch. Rustwick Northern Dancer, Ch. Rustwick Sir Einstein de Yame, Ch. Rustwick Nipsi Dancer, and Ch. Rustwick Rand Chianti.

San Su Kee Kennel, owned by Dorothy Palmerston of Minneapolis, Minnesota, has produced a consistent type of winner. Representatives of this breeding program are: Ch. San Su Kee Sunrise Serenade, Ch. San Su Kee Wendy of Course, Ch. San Su Kee Heir Extraordinair, and Ch. San Su Kee Chantilly Lace. Ch. San Su Kee Star Edition, co-owned with Richard Reid, is a Best-in-

Show winner as is Ch. San Su Kee Ring Leader Too, owned by Norman and Marjorie Nelson of Conquest Kennel.

Mrs. Margaret Spilling of Fort Lauderdale, Florida, is the owner of Shareen Kennel. This kennel's reputation rests not only on the record of its Maltese, but also on its Best-in-Show winning Yorkshire Terriers. Some of the winning Maltese are: Ch. Shareen Snow Flurry, Ch. Shareen Mr. Star Man, Ch. Shareen Sprig of Kelly, and Ch. Shareen Storm Star.

Mrs. Dolores Lewis of St. Louis, Missouri, is a professional handler. Her Spring Holly Kennel has won championship titles for both Maltese and Yorkshire Terriers. Mrs. Lewis co-owns a number of dogs with her sister-in-law, Mrs. Maurine Middleton. Group winning Ch. Spring Holly's Passin' Fancy was bred by Virginia Sunner Evans. Another winner is Ch. Spring Holly's Veri Meri.

A familiar figure in the show ring in the past dozen years is Frank Oberstar, who, with his partner Larry Ward of Euclid, Ohio, owned the great Ch. Aennchen's Poona Dancer. Poona, handled by Mr. Oberstar, is the top winning bitch in the history of the breed, with a total of thirty-eight Best-in-Show wins as well as a Best-of-Breed win at the 1967 American Maltese Association Specialty Show. Poona also won the Group at Westminster.

Other champions carrying Messrs. Oberstar and Ward's Starward Kennel title are Ch. Starward's Girlfriend, Ch. Starward's Bachelor Buttons, and Ch. Starward's Prince Valiant.

More than a dozen dogs have completed their championship under the Stentaway Kennel title. Included in this list are Ch. Stentaway's Sweetest Dancer, Ch. Stentaway's Gibson Girl, Ch. Stentaway's Sonny Boy, and Ch. Stentaway's Brag-A-Bout.

Small, typey Maltese carry the Su Le Kennel name into the show ring. Although breeding on a limited scale, Mrs. Barbara Berquist has finished twenty-five champions, including Ch. Su Le's Robin of Eng, Ch. Su Le's Bunting, Ch. Su Le's Meadow Lark, and Ch. Su Le's Roadrunner.

Mrs. Miriam Thompson of Sun Valley, California, has a list of champions that numbers more than fifty. Her Sun Canyon Kennel dogs have been active contenders in West Coast competition. Her great sire Ch. Indars King Midas has played a major role in establishing this remarkable record. The list of champions includes Ch. Sun Canyon the Bandit, Ch. The Maestro of Sun Canyon, Ch. Sun Canyon Double-O-Seven, Ch. Sun Canyon Show Stopper, and Ch. Sun Canyon Inca Idol. One of the recent Group winners is Ch. Sun Canyon Janelle.

Sunglow Kennel of Louisville, Kentucky, is the property of Mrs. Bessie Crowe. Mrs. Crowe has been interested in a number of different breeds through the years, and has finished champions in several of them. Lhasa Apsos have enjoyed special attention, along with the Maltese. Maltese winners include Ch. Sunglow's Beau and Ch. Sunglow's Tomi Too.

The West Park Kennel banner brought the following champions to their titles: Ch. West Park's Little White Queen, Ch. West Park's Snow Princess, and Ch. West Park's Little Zephyr.

Whispering Pine's Kennel of Mrs. H. W. Wilson had the pleasure of earning titles for Ch. Whispering Pine's Jennifer and Ch. Whispering Miss Brigitt.

Mrs. Vivian Horney of Miami, Florida, owns Winddrift Kennel. Winddrift dogs have been strong competitors in the ring and good representatives of the breed. Winners include Ch. Winddrift's Fantabulous, Ch. Winddrift's Sharazad, Ch. The Sarling of Winddrift, and Ch. Julie Ann of Winddrift.

Ch. Aennchen's Savar Dancer, owned by Mrs. J. P. Antonelli.

An 1892 steel engraving by T. Wood of Lady Giffard's Maltese Terrier "Hugh."

An 1881 lithograph of McJames Fawdry's Pomeranian "Charley" and Lady Giffard's Maltese "Hugh."

A steel engraving by T. Wood of Mr. R. Mandeville's Maltese Dog "Fido."

The Maltese in Other Countries

While the historical center for the Maltese may be on the island of Malta in the Mediterranean, it must be acknowledged that the development of the modern Maltese is credited to England. Although small lap dogs were generally popular throughout the courts of Renaissance Europe, it was not until well into the nineteenth century that they began to enjoy a popularity among a broader segment of the general population. Many countries took a special pride in developing their own particular breed that has since become identified as a national breed.

The Maltese was first shown in the Miscellaneous Class in England. When recognition was eventually given to the breed so that it could be shown in regular championship competition, it was placed in the Utility or Non-Sporting Group. It was not until 1947 that the Maltese was transferred to the Toy Group, where it remains at present.

Provisions were made by the English Kennel Club in 1886 to show white Maltese in competition at championship shows. Starting in 1902, permission was granted to show colored Maltese weighing up to twelve pounds. It was not, however, until 1908 that the colored Maltese were allowed to compete in championship shows. The colored Maltese are undoubtedly the product of the Shih Tzu-Maltese crosses made in the Orient and discussed under "History of the Maltese."

Records of the English Kennel Club indicate that the first individual registration of a Maltese took place at a match held in London in 1859. This first dog was Psyche. Popularity of the breed grew, and by 1862 there was an entry of twenty Maltese at another show held in the capital.

The first Maltese to establish a record of show wins was Fido, who was owned by Mr. Robert Mandeville. By present day standards, Fido was a moderately short-backed dog with modest coat. He had a long show career, extending from 1863 to 1870.

The second Maltese to gain stature in the show ring was Hugh, owned by Lady Giffard. Hugh was longer backed than Fido and, from etchings of the period, appears to have had a curlier coat—a quality that has been identified with many of the English Maltese. Hugh lived to be fourteen years old and died in 1886. It is most interesting to note that he was still being entered in show competition when he was thirteen years old. This record has probably never been duplicated.

Many of the kennels that gained fame for the breeding of quality Maltese did not originally establish their kennel with this breed. It was the second, third, and in some cases even the fourth breed in a kennel. Many of these breeders started with larger breeds, shifting at a later date to the Toy Maltese.

Invicta Kennel, established and owned by Mrs. M. M. Neame, holds a record not likely to be broken. For over forty years, from the 1920s until the 1960s, Invicta was dedicated to the breeding of quality Maltese. These dogs not only gained outstanding recognition in England, but also were exported to many foreign countries where they carried the name Invicta into the winner's circle. Scores of Invicta-bred Maltese have gained championship titles throughout the world, so it would be impossible to include a list of all the winners. However, it is possible to record a few of the early winners who appear in so many of the winning pedigrees. Among the greats were Ch. Invicta Quixotic, Ch. Invicta Dollar, Ch. Invicta Demetrius, and Ch. Invicta Periwinkle.

Mrs. C. Roberts established her Harlingen Kennel in the 1920s. To give breadth to her line and to bring in new blood, Mrs. Roberts imported a number of Maltese from Germany. This combination of bloodlines produced such champions as Harlingen Emblem and the great Ch. Harlingen Snowman. Snowman established an incredible record in the 1930s by earning seventeen Challenge Certificates. This record still stands today as one of the greatest in the breed. Ch. Harlingen May Bloom was shipped to Ceylon, where he went Best in Show.

Fawkhan Kennel was established by Miss Betty Worthington in the 1930s. Among her great Maltese are Ch. Nicholas of Fawkhan and Ch. Christopher of Fawkhan. Miss Worthington exported her dogs all over the world. These dogs were especially prized in Italy, where they served as foundation stock for several outstanding kennels.

World War II understandably had a great effect on the dog world of England. Many kennels were completely disbanded while others cut back greatly on their breeding programs. Following the war, however, there was a resurgence of interest in the breeding of quality Maltese.

Mrs. Marian Crook of Skye Terrier fame has bred numerous champion Maltese under her Rhosneigr Kennel name. This kennel, established in the 1940s, has produced such winners as Ch. Rhosneigr Sweetheart and Ch. Rhosneigr Beau Brummel.

Leckhampton Kennel, also established in the 1940s, is owned by Mrs. I. C. Brierley. Leckhampton Kennel not only is credited with a number of champions in England, but also has exported numerous dogs that have gained championship titles in other countries. Leckhampton Sprig, for example, was exported to the United States, where he completed his championship. He is now owned by Mrs. Roberta Harrison of Bobbelee Kennel.

Mrs. C. M. Hunter originally established her Gissing Kennel in England in the 1940s. She has since moved to Portugal, where she continues her breeding program. Among her winning dogs are Ch. Spaceman of Gissing, Ch. Singing Elf of Gissing, and Ch. Gay Starlight of Gissing. Gissing Kennel has also exported numerous Maltese to the United States, where they have completed their championship. Ch. Ailos of Gissing, exported to France, accumulated eight CACIB's, ten CACS, one RCACIB, and one RCAC in France, Belgium, Luxembourg, Germany, and Monaco.

Vicbrita Kennel has long been a favorite of both English and American breeders. Mrs. Margaret White established her breeding line in the 1950s. The following winners are representative of her breeding: Ch. Vicbrita Pimpernel; his son Ch. Vicbrita Fidelity, a Best-in-Show winner with fifteen CC's; and Ch. Vicbrita Delight.

Also established in the 1950s was Yelwa Kennel belonging to Mrs. Blanche Mace. Among her winners are Ch. Jacques of Yelwa, Ch. Shamus of Yelwa, and International Ch. Avyola of Yelwa.

Between 1950 and the mid 1960s, Mrs. Joan Felice bred a number of show-winning Maltese under the Suirside prefix. Two outstanding examples are Ch. Lionheart of Suirside and Ch. Aurora of Suirside. Many Maltese were shipped to the United States from this kennel, which is based in Ireland.

In the 1970s, Ellwin Kennel of Mrs. Muriel Kent is enjoying national recognition with the Best-in-Show Ch. Ellwin Sue Ellen, who went B.O.B. at Cruft's in 1973. Other winners are Ch. Ellwin Marquiss and English and American Ch. Ellwin Mari Anna.

While it is difficult to generalize about breeding strains, it is possible to make a few observations about the Maltese of England. In comparison to the Maltese now being bred in the United States, the Maltese of England are somewhat larger and seem to have longer

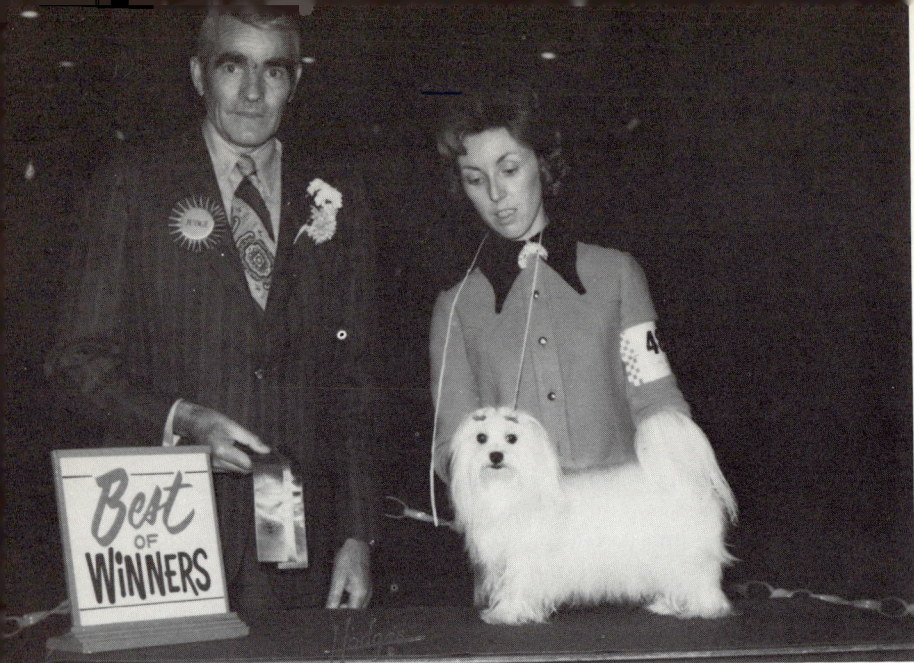

Can Ch. Cotterell's Miss Canada, owned by Maureen Bannen.

Ch. Good Time Hilda, owned by the Author and shown by John Struwe.

muzzles. Coats, while dense and long, at times have a tendency to be somewhat curly. There are, of course, many examples that do not fall within these generalizations. That there is a growing difference in the Maltese of the United States and England is attested by the fact that fewer specimens are being imported from England than in the past. Those that are being imported at present do not seem to be enjoying the success in the ring that earlier imports did.

The title of champion in England is not based on a point system as it is in the United States. The winning of three Challenge Certificates under three different judges entitles a dog to be called champion. The number of CC's to be awarded each year is established by the English Kennel Club on a nation-wide basis. The number of certificates awarded to any breed is based on the average registration per year on a three-year basis. The following schedule for the allocation of CC's has been adopted by the English Kennel Club effective in 1975:

Three-Year Registration	Total CC's
up to 200	up to 8
201-300	11
301-500	13
501-800	16
801-1,000	18
1,001-1,500	20
1,501-1,800	22
1,801-2,500	24

Provisions are made for registrations of up to 50,000, for which forty-four CC's are awarded. Such large numbers are unlikely ever to be of significance to Maltese breeders, for average registrations number in the hundreds rather than in the thousands.

Early Canadian kennels, like those of the United States, acquired their foundation stock from English kennels. Initial interest was manifested in Canada in the early 1900s, but it was not until World War I that the Maltese began to enjoy general recognition and popularity. In addition to stock imported from England, numerous dogs were purchased in the United States and brought back to Canada. The Kennel Club of Canada awarded its first Maltese championship title to Highbury Snow Ball in 1915.

A few years back, Miss Mary Annand finished her Irish import, Brigid of Suirside, to title. Another winner in the mid 1960s, not only in Canada but also in the United States, was International Ch. Poodhall Diana of Mar-a-Nor, owned by Mrs. Jane Morgan.

Another of Mrs. Morgan's home-breds was Diana's brother, American and Canadian Ch. Poodhall Euripides. Ch. Poodhall Demosthenes is still another winner. Mrs. Morgan purchased her foundation stock from Villa Malta Kennels.

Other Canadian breeders and exhibitors include: Mrs. J. Brian Aune, Montreal, Quebec; Mrs. Marguerite Barfeider, Ottawa, Ontario; Remi Charset, Edmonton, Alberta; Fred Kramer, West Vancouver, British Columbia; Mrs. Evan Stanley, New Westminster, British Columbia: and Mrs. R. G. Stapley, Willowdale, Ontario.

The Maltese has been a popular breed in Italy since the times of the Romans. Their great popularity is suggested by their frequent representation in Renaissance paintings, tapestries, and pottery. The Maltese was exhibited in the Miscellaneous Class in the early 1900s before being transferred to the Toy Group.

Mrs. Nadya Colombo established her Electa Kennel in 1930 and operated it into the 1950s. Her original stock was purchased from Invicta Kennel in England. Such winners as Ch. Electa Brio, Ch. Electa Petin, Ch. Electa Fiorella, and Ch. Electa Cinzia not only influenced the present day Maltese in Italy, but also those in the United States. This influence in the United States came through the Electa dogs that Dr. Vicenzo Calvaresi imported for his Villa Malta Kennel. These dogs excelled in head and coat and passed these qualities down through many generations of American-bred dogs.

Ms. Bianca Tamagnone established her Gemma Kennel in Italy in the early 1950s. For her foundation stock she purchased dogs from Electa Kennel and also from Vicbrita Kennel in England. The crossbreeding of the Electa line with the Vicbrita line produced a slightly different type from that resulting from the Electa-Invicta cross.

While the Maltese has never enjoyed the great popularity in France that it did either in England or in Italy, it is a recognized breed and was accepted for registration as early as 1923. The French name for the Maltese is *Bichons Maltais et Havanasi*. This breed is entered in Group competition under *Chien de Dame*, which, translated, means Lady's Dog, giving further evidence of the appeal of Toy dogs to the ladies.

In Germany the Maltese or *Malteser* was accepted for studbook registration in the early 1900s. He is exhibited in Group V under the title of House and Miniature Dogs. The general popularity of the Maltese is not much greater in Germany than it is in France.

Since World War II, the Japanese have exhibited ever increasing interest in purebred dogs in general and in the Maltese in particular. With a rapidly expanding economy resulting in a growing affluent society and a large supply of low-salaried kennel help, the Japanese are able to maintain their dogs in first-rate show coats at all times.

The Japanese imported dogs both from England and from the United States in quantities during the late 1950s and throughout the 1960s. From England came Ch. Lord Pamplemouse of Gissing, while from the United States, A-S Gloria's Kennel of M. Akira Shinohara imported Ch. Joanne-Chen's Shikar Dancer and Ch. Joanne-Chen's Sweet He Dancer, both of whom have left their mark on the present day Maltese of Japan.

Other breeder-exhibitors from Japan include Tatsuo Kasai of Ota-Ku, Tokyo, and Mrs. Fusae Amemori of Hiroshima.

In the Republic of South Africa, C. D. Overturf represents the interest of the Maltese, while in Spain, Señor Favier Llana brings interest to the breed with his Spanish and International Ch. Francoombe Pipelac.

Brazilian Ch. Marenacass Maytheas Sincerely, owned by Nair Freire Nohe.

Ch. Su-Le's Wren of Eng, owned by
Barbara Berquist.

Ch. Spring Holly's Veri Meri, owned by
Delores Lewis and Maurine Middleton.

Ch. Joanne-Chen's Sweetest Dancer,
owned by Dr. & Mrs. Nelson King.

Manners for
the Family Dog

Although each dog has personality quirks and idiosyncrasies that set him apart as an individual, dogs in general have two characteristics that can be utilized to advantage in training. The first is the dog's strong desire to please, which has been built up through centuries of association with man. The second lies in the innate quality of the dog's mentality. It has been proved conclusively that while dogs have reasoning power, their learning ability is based on a direct association of cause and effect, so that they willingly repeat acts that bring pleasant results and discontinue acts that bring unpleasant results. Hence, to take fullest advantage of a dog's abilities, the trainer must make sure the dog understands a command, and then reward him when he obeys and correct him when he does wrong.

Commands should be as short as possible and should be repeated in the same way, day after day. Saying "Heel," one day, and "Come here and heel," the next will confuse the dog. *Heel, sit, stand, stay, down,* and *come* are standard terminology, and are preferable for a dog that may later be given advanced training.

Tone of voice is important, too. For instance, a coaxing tone helps cajole a young puppy into trying something new. Once an exercise is mastered, commands given in a firm, matter-of-fact voice give the dog confidence in his own ability. Praise, expressed in an exuberant tone will tell the dog quite clearly that he has earned his master's approval. On the other hand, a firm "No" indicates with equal clarity that he has done wrong.

Rewards for good performance may consist simply of praising lavishly and petting the dog, although many professional trainers use bits of food as rewards. Tidbits are effective only if the dog is hungry, of course. And if you smoke, you must be sure to wash your hands before each training session, for the odor of nicotine is repulsive to dogs. On the hands of a heavy smoker, the odor of nicotine may be so strong that the dog is unable to smell the tidbit.

Correction for wrong-doing should be limited to repeating "No," in a scolding tone of voice or to confining the dog to his bed. Spanking or striking the dog is taboo—particularly using sticks, which might cause injury, but the hand should never be used either. For field training as well as some obedience work, the hand is used to signal the dog. Dogs that have been punished by slapping have a tendency to cringe whenever they see a hand raised and consequently do not respond promptly when the owner's intent is not to punish but to signal.

Some trainers recommend correcting the dog by whacking him with a rolled-up newspaper. The idea is that the newspaper will not injure the dog but that the resulting noise will condition the dog to avoid repeating the act that seemingly caused the noise. Many authorities object to this type of correction, for it may result in the dog's becoming "noise-shy"—a decided disadvantage with show dogs which must maintain poise in adverse, often noisy, situations. "Noise-shyness" is also an unfortunate reaction in field dogs, since it may lead to gun-shyness.

To be effective, correction must be administered immediately, so that in the dog's mind there is a direct connection between his act and the correction. You can make voice corrections under almost any circumstances, but you must never call the dog to you and then correct him, or he will associate the correction with the fact that he has come and will become reluctant to respond. If the dog is at a distance and doing something he shouldn't, go to him and scold him while he is still involved in wrong-doing. If this is impossible, ignore the offense until he repeats it and you can correct him properly.

Especially while a dog is young, he should be watched closely and stopped before he gets into mischief. All dogs need to do a certain amount of chewing, so to prevent your puppy's chewing something you value, provide him with his own rubber balls and toys. Never allow him to chew cast-off slippers and then expect him to differentiate between cast-off items and those you value. Nylon stockings, wooden articles, and various other items may cause intestinal obstructions if the dog chews and swallows them, and death may result. So it is essential that the dog be permitted to chew only on bones or rubber toys.

Serious training for obedience should not be started until a dog is a year old. But basic training in house manners should begin the day the puppy enters his new home. A puppy should never be given the run of the house but should be confined to a box or small pen except for play periods when you can devote full attention to him. The first thing to teach the dog is his name, so that whenever he hears it, he will immediately come to attention. Whenever you are near his box, talk to him, using his name repeatedly. During play periods, talk to him, pet him, and handle him, for he must be conditioned so he will not object to being handled by a veterinarian, show judge, or family friend. As the dog investigates his surroundings, watch him carefully and if he tries something he shouldn't, reprimand him with a scolding "No!" If he repeats the offense, scold him and confine him to his box, then praise him. Discipline must be prompt, consistent, and always followed with praise. Never tease the dog, and never allow others to do so. Kindness and understanding are essential to a pleasant, mutually rewarding relationship.

When the puppy is two to three months old, secure a flat, narrow leather collar and have him start wearing it (never use a harness, which will encourage tugging and pulling). After a week or so, attach a light leather lead to the collar during play sessions and let the puppy walk around, dragging the lead behind him. Then start holding the end of the lead and coaxing the puppy to come to you. He will then be fully accustomed to collar and lead when you start taking him outside while he is being housebroken.

Housebreaking can be accomplished in a matter of approximately two weeks provided you wait until the dog is mature enough to have some control over bodily functions. This is usually at about four months. Until that time, the puppy should spend most of his day confined to his penned area, with the floor covered with several thicknesses of newspapers so that he may relieve himself when necessary without damage to floors.

Either of two methods works well in housebreaking—the choice depending upon where you live. If you live in a house with a readily accessible yard, you will probably want to train the puppy from the beginning to go outdoors. If you live in an apartment without easy access to a yard, you may decide to train him first to relieve himself on newspapers and then when he has learned control, to teach the puppy to go outdoors.

If you decide to train the puppy by taking him outdoors, arrange some means of confining him indoors where you can watch him closely—in a small penned area, or tied to a short lead (five or six feet). Dogs are naturally clean animals, reluctant to soil their quarters, and confining the puppy to a limited area will encourage him to avoid making a mess.

A young puppy must be taken out often, so watch your puppy closely and if he indicates he is about to relieve himself, take him out at once. If he has an accident, scold him and take him out so he will associate the act of going outside with the need to relieve himself. Always take the puppy out within an hour after meals—preferably to the same place each time—and make sure he relieves himself before you return him to the house. Restrict his water for two hours before bedtime and take him out just before you retire for the night. Then, as soon as you wake in the morning, take him out again.

For paper training, set aside a particular room and cover a large area of the floor with several thicknesses of newspapers. Confine the dog on a short leash and each time he relieves himself, remove the soiled papers and replace them with clean ones.

As his control increases, gradually decrease the paper area, leaving part of the floor bare. If he uses the bare floor, scold him mildly and put him on the papers, letting him know that there is where he is to relieve himself. As he comes to understand the idea, increase the bare area until papers cover only space equal to approximately two full newspaper sheets. Keep him using the papers, but begin taking him on a leash to the street at the times of day that he habitually relieves himself. Watch him closely when he is indoors and at the first sign that he needs to go, take him outdoors. Restrict his water for two hours before bedtime, but if necessary, permit him to use the papers before you retire for the night.

Using either method, the puppy will be housebroken in an amazingly short time. Once he has learned control he will need to relieve himself only four or five times a day.

Informal obedience training, started at the age of about six to eight months, will provide a good background for any advanced training you may decide to give your dog later. The collar most

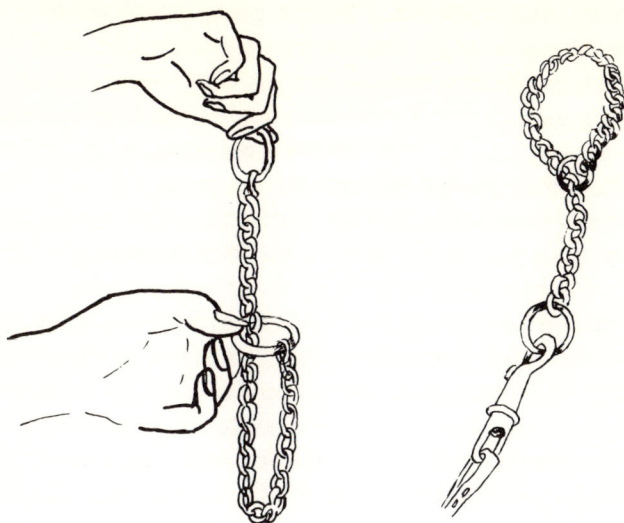

effective for training is the metal chain-link variety. The correct size for your dog will be about one inch longer than the measurement around the largest part of his head. The chain must be slipped through one of the rings so the collar forms a loop. The collar should be put on with the loose ring at the right of the dog's neck, the chain attached to it coming over the neck and through the holding ring, rather than under the neck. Since the dog is to be at your left during most of the training, this makes the collar most effective.

The leash should be attached to the loose ring, and should be either webbing or leather, six feet long and a half inch to a full inch wide. When you want your dog's attention, or wish to correct him, give a light, quick pull on the leash, which will momentarily tighten the collar about the neck. Release the pressure instantly, and the correction will have been made. If the puppy is already accustomed to a leather collar, he will adjust easily to the training collar. But before you start training sessions, practice walking with the dog until he responds readily when you increase tension on the leash.

Set aside a period of fifteen minutes, once or twice a day, for regular training sessions, and train in a place where there will be no distractions. Teach only one exercise at a time, making sure the dog has mastered it before going on to another. It will probably take at least a week for the dog to master each exercise. As training progresses, start each session by reviewing exercises the dog has already learned, then go on to the new exercise for a period of concerted practice. When discipline is required, make the correction immediately, and always praise the dog after corrections as well as when he obeys promptly. During each session stick strictly to business. Afterwards, take time to play with the dog.

The first exercise to teach is heeling. Have the dog at your left and hold the leash as shown in the illustration on the preceding page. Start walking, and just as you put your foot forward for the first step, say your dog's name to get his attention, followed by the command, "Heel!" Simultaneously, pull on the leash lightly. As you walk, try to keep the dog at your left side, with his head alongside your left leg. Pull on the leash as necessary to urge him forward or back, to right or left, but keep him in position. Each time you pull on the leash, say "Heel!" and praise the dog lavishly. When the dog heels properly in a straight line, start making circles, turning corners, etc.

Once the dog has learned to heel well, start teaching the "sit." Each time you stop while heeling, command "Sit!" The dog will be at your left, so use your left hand to press on his rear and guide him to a sitting position, while you use the leash in your right hand to keep his head up. Hold him in position for a few moments while you praise him, then give the command to heel. Walk a few steps, stop, and repeat the procedure. Before long he will automatically sit whenever you stop. You can then teach the dog to "sit" from any position.

When the dog will sit on command without correction, he is ready to learn to stay until you release him. Simply sit him, command "Stay!" and hold him in position for perhaps half a minute, repeating "Stay," if he attempts to stand. You can release him by saying "O.K." Gradually increase the time until he will stay on command for three or four minutes.

The "stand-stay" should also be taught when the dog is on leash. While you are heeling, stop and give the command "Stand!" Keep the dog from sitting by quickly placing your left arm under him, immediately in front of his right hind leg. If he continues to try to sit, don't scold him but start up again with the heel command, walk a few steps, and stop again, repeating the stand command and preventing the dog from sitting. Once the dog has mastered the stand, teach him to stay by holding him in position and repeating the word "Stay!"

The "down stay" will prove beneficial in many situations, but especially if you wish to take your dog in the car without confining him to a crate. To teach the "down," have the dog sitting at your side with collar and leash on. If he is a large dog, step forward with the leash in your hand and turn so you face him. Let the leash touch the floor, then step over it with your right foot so it is under the instep of your shoe. Grasping the leash low down with both hands, slowly pull up, saying, "Down!" Hold the leash taut until the dog goes down. Once he responds well, teach the dog to stay in the down position (the down-stay), using the same method as for the sit- and stand-stays.

To teach small dogs the "down," another method may be used. Have the dog sit at your side, then kneel beside him. Reach across his back with your left arm, and take hold of his left front leg close to the body. At the same time, with your right hand take hold of his right front leg close to his body. As you command "Down!" gently lift the legs and place the dog in the down position. Release your hold on his legs and slide your left hand onto his back, repeating, "Down, stay," while keeping him in position.

The "come" is taught when the dog is on leash and heeling. Simply walk along, then suddenly take a step backward, saying "Come!" Pull the leash as you give the command and the dog will turn and follow you. Continue walking backward, repeatedly saying "Come," and tightening the leash if necessary.

Once the dog has mastered the exercises while on leash, try taking the leash off and going through the same routine, beginning with the heeling exercise. If the dog doesn't respond promptly, he needs review with the leash on. But patience and persistence will be rewarded, for you will have a dog you can trust to respond promptly under all conditions.

Even after they are well trained, dogs sometimes develop bad habits that are hard to break. Jumping on people is a common habit, and all members of the family must assist if it is to be broken. If the dog is a large or medium breed, take a step forward and raise your knee just as he starts to jump on you. As your knee strikes the dog's chest, command "Down!" in a scolding voice. When a small dog jumps on you, take both front paws in your hands, and, while talking in a pleasant tone of voice, step on the dog's back feet just hard enough to hurt them slightly. With either method the dog is taken by surprise and doesn't associate the discomfort with the person causing it.

Occasionally a dog may be too chummy with guests who don't care for dogs. If the dog has had obedience training, simply command "Come!" When he responds, have him sit beside you.

Excessive barking is likely to bring complaints from neighbors, and persistent efforts may be needed to subdue a dog that barks without provocation. To correct the habit, you must be close to the dog when he starts barking. Encircle his muzzle with both hands, hold his mouth shut, and command "Quiet!" in a firm voice. He should soon learn to respond so you can control him simply by giving the command.

Sniffing other dogs is an annoying habit. If the dog is off leash and sniffs other dogs, ignoring your commands to come, he needs to review the lessons on basic behavior. When the dog is on leash, scold him, then pull on the leash, command "Heel," and walk away from the other dog.

A well-trained dog will be no problem if you decide to take him with you when you travel. No matter how well he responds, however, he should never be permitted off leash when you walk him in a strange area. Distractions will be more tempting, and there will be more chance of his being attacked by other dogs. So whenever the dog travels with you, take his collar and leash along—and use them.

Bench Shows

Centuries ago, it was common practice to hold agricultural fairs in conjunction with spring and fall religious festivals, and to these gatherings, cattle, dogs, and other livestock were brought for exchange. As time went on, it became customary to provide entertainment, too. Dogs often participated in such sporting events as bull baiting, bear baiting, and ratting. Then the dog that exhibited the greatest skill in the arena was also the one that brought the highest price when time came for barter or sale. To-day, these fairs seem a far cry from our highly organized bench shows and field trials. But they were the forerunners of modern dog shows and played an important role in shaping the development of purebred dogs.

The first organized dog show was held at Newcastle, England, in 1859. Later that same year, a show was held at Birmingham. At both shows dogs were divided into four classes and only Pointers and Setters were entered. In 1860, the first dog show in Germany was held at Apoldo, where nearly one hundred dogs were exhibited and entries were divided into six groups. Interest expanded rapidly, and by the time the Paris Exhibition was held in 1878, the dog show was a fixture of international importance.

In the United States, the first organized bench show was held in 1874 in conjunction with the meeting of the Illinois State Sportsmen's Association in Chicago, and all entries were dogs of sporting breeds. Although the show was a rather casual affair, interest spread quickly. Before the end of the year, shows were held in Oswego, New York, Mineola, Long Island, and Memphis, Tennessee. And the latter combined a bench show with the first organized field trial ever held in the United States. In January 1875, an all-breed show (the first in the United States) was held at Detroit, Michigan. From then on, interest increased rapidly, though rules were not always uniform, for there was no organization through which to coordinate activities until September 1884

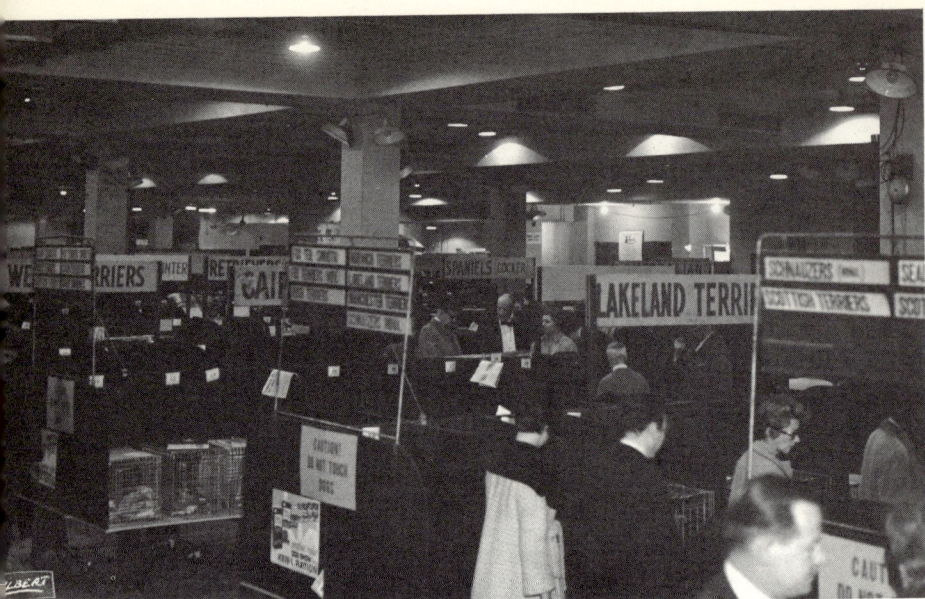

Benching area at Westminster Kennel Club Show.

Judging for Best in Show at Westminster Kennel Club Show.

when The American Kennel Club was founded. Now the largest dog registering organization in the world, the A.K.C. is an association of several hundred member clubs—all breed, specialty, field trial, and obedience groups—each represented by a delegate to the A.K.C.

The several thousand shows and trials held annually in the United States do much to stimulate interest in breeding to produce better looking, sounder, purebred dogs. For breeders, shows provide a means of measuring the merits of their work as compared with accomplishments of other breeders. For hundreds of thousands of dog fanciers, they provide an absorbing hobby.

For both spectators and participating owners, field trials constitute a fascinating demonstration of dogs competing under actual hunting conditions, where emphasis is on excellence of performance. The trials are sponsored by clubs or associations of persons interested in hunting dogs. Trials for Pointing breeds, Dachshunds, Retrievers, Spaniels, and Beagles are under the jurisdiction of The American Kennel Club and information concerning such activities is published in "Pure Bred Dogs—American Kennel Gazette." Trials for Bird Dogs are run by rules and regulations of the Amateur Field Trial Clubs of America and information concerning them is published in "The American Field."

All purebred dogs of recognized breeds may be registered with The American Kennel Club and those of hunting breeds may also be registered with The American Field. Dogs that have won championships both in the field and in bench shows are known as dual champions.

At bench (or conformation) shows, dogs are rated comparatively on their physical qualities (or conformation) in accordance with breed Standards which have been approved by The American Kennel Club. Characteristics such as size, coat, color, placement of eye or ear, general soundness, etc., are the basis for selecting the best dog in a class. Only purebred dogs are eligible to compete and if the show is one where points toward a championship are to be awarded, a dog must be at least six months old.

Bench shows are of various types. An all-breed show has classes for all of the breeds recognized by The American Kennel Club as well as a Miscellaneous Class for breeds not recognized, such as the Australian Cattle Dog, the Ibizan Hound, the Spinoni Italiani, the Tibetan Terrier, etc. A sanctioned match is an informal meeting where dogs compete but not for championship points. A specialty show is confined to a single breed. Other shows may restrict entries to champions of record, to American-bred dogs, etc. Competition for Junior Showmanship or for Best Brace, Best Team, or Best Local Dog may be included. Also, obedience competition is held in conjunction with many bench shows.

The term "bench show" is somewhat confusing in that shows of this type may be either "benched" or "unbenched." At the former, each dog is assigned an individual numbered stall where he must remain throughout the show except for times when he is being judged, groomed, or exercised. At unbenched shows, no stalls are provided and dogs are kept in their owners' cars or in crates when not being judged.

A show where a dog is judged for conformation actually constitutes an elimination contest. To begin with, the dogs of a single breed compete with others of their breed in one of the regular classes: Puppy, Novice, Bred by Exhibitor, American-Bred, or Open, and, finally, Winners, where the top dogs of the preceding five classes meet. The next step is the judging for Best of Breed (or Best of Variety of Breed). Here the Winners Dog and Winners Bitch (or the dog named Winners if only one prize is awarded) compete with any champions that are entered, together with any undefeated dogs that have competed in additional non-regular classes. The dog named Best of Breed (or Best of Variety of Breed), then goes on to compete with the other Best of Breed winners in his Group. The dogs that win in Group competition then compete for the final and highest honor, Best in Show.

When the Winners Class is divided by sex, championship points are awarded the Winners Dog and Winners Bitch. If the Winners Class is not divided by sex, championship points are awarded the dog or bitch named Winners. The number of points awarded varies, depending upon such factors as the number of dogs competing, the Schedule of Points established by the Board of Directors of the A.K.C., and whether the dog goes on to win Best of Breed, the Group, and Best in Show.

In order to become a champion, a dog must win fifteen points, including points from at least two major wins—that is, at least two shows where three or more points are awarded. The major wins must be under two different judges, and one or more of the remaining points must be won under a third judge. The most points ever awarded at a show is five and the least is one, so, in order to become

Junior Showmanship Competition at Westminster Kennel Club Show.

a champion, a dog must be exhibited and win in at least three shows, and usually he is shown many times before he wins his championship.

"Pure Bred Dogs—American Kennel Gazette" and other dog magazines contain lists of forthcoming shows, together with names and addresses of sponsoring organizations to which you may write for entry forms and information relative to fees, closing dates, etc. Before entering your dog in a show for the first time, you should familiarize yourself with the regulations and rules governing competition. You may secure such information from The American Kennel Club or from a local dog club specializing in your breed. It is essential that you also familiarize yourself with the A.K.C. approved Standard for your breed so you will be fully aware of characteristics worthy of merit as well as those considered faulty, or possibly even serious enough to disqualify the dog from competition. For instance, monorchidism (failure of one testicle to descend) and cryptorchidism (failure of both testicles to descend) are disqualifying faults in all breeds.

If possible, you should first attend a show as a spectator and observe judging procedures from ringside. It will also be helpful to join a local breed club and to participate in sanctioned matches before entering an all-breed show.

The dog should be equipped with a narrow leather show lead and a show collar—never an ornamented or spiked collar. For benched shows, a metal-link bench chain will be needed to fasten the dog to the bench. For unbenched shows, the dog's crate should be taken along so that he may be confined in comfort when he is not appearing in the ring. A dog should never be left in a car with all the windows closed. In hot weather the temperature will become unbearable in a very short time. Heat exhaustion may result from even a short period of confinement, and death may ensue.

Food and water dishes will be needed, as well as a supply of the food and water to which the dog is accustomed. Brushes and combs are also necessary, so that you may give the dog's coat a final grooming after you arrive at the show.

Familiarize yourself with the schedule of classes ahead of time, for the dog must be fed and exercised and permitted to relieve himself, and any last-minute grooming completed before his class is called. Both you and the dog should be ready to enter the ring unhurriedly. A good deal of skill in conditioning, training, and handling is required if a dog is to be presented properly. And it is essential that the handler himself be composed, for a jittery handler will transmit his nervousness to his dog.

Once the class is assembled in the ring, the judge will ask that the dogs be paraded in line, moving counter-clockwise in a circle. If you have trained your dog well, you will have no difficulty controlling him in the ring, where he must change pace quickly and gracefully and walk and trot elegantly and proudly with head erect. The show dog must also stand quietly for inspection, posing like a statue for several minutes while the judge observes his structure in detail, examines teeth, feet, coat, etc. When the judge calls your dog forward for individual inspection, do not attempt to converse, but answer any questions he may ask.

As the judge examines the class, he measures each dog against the ideal described in the Standard, then measures the dogs against each other in a comparative sense and selects for first place the dog that comes closest to conforming to the Standard for its breed. If your dog isn't among the winners, don't grumble. If he places first, don't brag loudly. For a bad loser is disgusting, but a poor winner is insufferable.

Obedience Competition

For hundreds of years, dogs have been used in England and Germany in connection with police and guard work, and their working potential has been evaluated through tests devised to show agility, strength, and courage. Organized training has also been popular with English and German breeders for many years, although it was first practiced primarily for the purpose of training large breeds in aggressive tactics.

There was little interest in obedience training in the United States until 1933 when Mrs. Whitehouse Walker returned from England and enthusiastically introduced the sport. Two years later, Mrs. Walker persuaded The American Kennel Club to approve organized obedience activities and to assume jurisdiction over obedience rules. Since then, interest has increased at a phenomenal rate, for obedience competition is not only a sport the average spectator can follow readily, but also a sport for which the average owner can train his own dog easily. Obedience competition is suitable for all breeds. Furthermore, there is no limit to the number of dogs that may win in competition, for each dog is scored individually on the basis of a point rating system.

The dog is judged on his response to certain commands, and if he gains a high enough score in three successive trials under different judges, he wins an obedience degree. Degrees awarded are "C.D."—Companion Dog; "C.D.X."—Companion Dog Excellent; and "U.D."—Utility Dog. A fourth degree, the "T.D.," or Tracking Dog degree, may be won at any time and tests for it are held apart from dog shows. The qualifying score is a minimum of 170 points out of a possible total of 200, with no score in any one exercise less than 50% of the points allotted.

Since obedience titles are progressive, earlier titles (with the exception of the tracking degree) are dropped as a dog acquires the next higher degree. If an obedience title is gained in another country in addition to the United States, that fact is signified by the word "International," followed by the title.

Trials for obedience trained dogs are held at most of the larger bench shows, and obedience training clubs are to be found in almost all communities today. Information concerning forthcoming trials and lists of obedience training clubs are included regularly in "Pure Bred Dogs—American Kennel Gazette"—and other dog magazines. Pamphlets containing rules and regulations governing obedience competition are available upon request from The American Kennel Club, 51 Madison Avenue, New York, N.Y. 10010. Rules are revised occasionally, so if you are interested in participating in obedience competition, you should be sure your copy of the regulations is current.

All dogs must comply with the same rules, although in broad jump, high jump, and bar jump competition, the jumps are adjusted to the size of the breed. Classes at obedience trials are divided into Novice (A and B), Open (A and B), and Utility (which may be divided into A and B, at the option of the sponsoring club and with the approval of The American Kennel Club).

The Novice class is for dogs that have not won the title Companion Dog. In Novice A, no person who has previously handled a dog that has won a C.D. title in the obedience ring at a licensed or member trial, and no person who has regularly trained such a dog, may enter or handle a dog. The handler must be the dog's owner or a member of the owner's immediate family. In Novice B, dogs may be handled by the owner or any other person.

The Open A class is for dogs that have won the C.D. title but have not won the C.D.X. title. Obedience judges and licensed handlers may not enter or handle dogs in this class. Each dog must be handled by the owner or by a member of his immediate family. The Open B class is for dogs that have won the title C.D. or C.D.X. A dog may continue to compete in this class after it has won the title U.D. Dogs in this class may be handled by the owner or any other person.

The Utility class is for dogs that have won the title C.D.X. Dogs that have won the title U.D. may continue to compete in this class, and dogs may be handled by the owner or any other person. Provided the A.K.C. approves, a club may choose to divide the Utility class into Utility A and Utility B. When this is done, the Utility A class is for dogs that have won the title C.D.X. and have not won the title U.D. Obedience judges and licensed handlers may not enter or handle dogs in this class. All other dogs that are eligible for the Utility class but not eligible for Utility A may be entered in Utility B.

Novice competition includes such exercises as heeling on and off lead, the stand for examination, coming on recall, and the long sit and the long down.

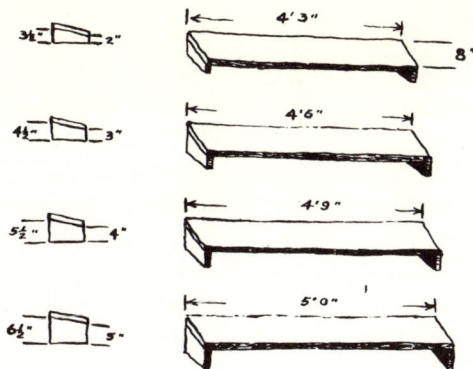

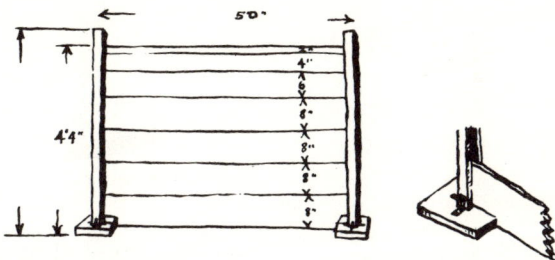

Broad jump and solid hurdle.

In Open competition, the dog must perform such exercises as heeling free, the drop on recall, and the retrieve on the flat and over the high jump. Also, he must execute the broad jump, and the long sit and long down.

In the Utility class, competition includes scent discrimination, the directed retrieve, the signal exercise, directed jumping, and the group examination.

Tracking is the most difficult test. It is always done out-of-doors, of course, and, for obvious reasons, cannot be held at a dog show. The dog must follow a scent trail that is about a quarter mile in length. He is also required to find a scent object (glove, wallet, or other article) left by a stranger who has walked the course to lay down the scent. The dog is required to follow the trail a half to two hours after the scent is laid.

An ideal way to train a dog for obedience competition is to join an obedience class or a training club. In organized class work, beginners' classes cover pretty much the same exercises as those

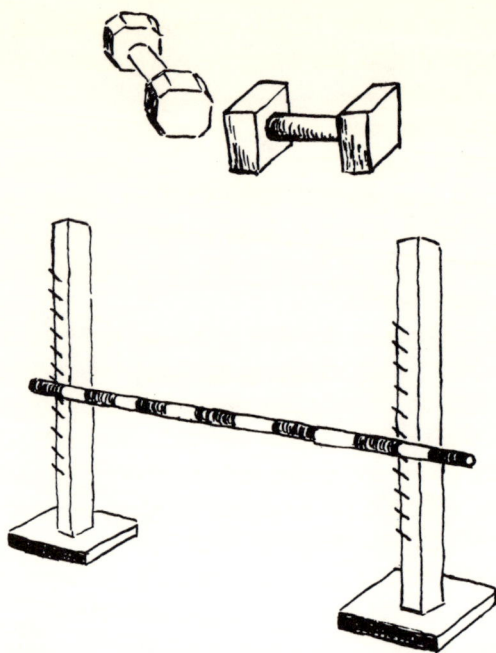

Dumbbells and bar jump.

described in the chapter on training. However, through class work you will develop greater precision than is possible in training your dog by yourself. Amateur handlers often cause the dog to be penalized, for if the handler fails to abide by the rules, it is the dog that suffers the penalty. A common infraction of the rules is using more than one signal or command where regulations stipulate only one may be used. Classwork will help eliminate such errors, which the owner may make unconsciously if he is working alone. Working with a class will also acquaint both dog and handler with ring procedure so that obedience trials will not present unforeseen problems.

Thirty or forty owners and dogs often comprise a class, and exercises are performed in unison, with individual instruction provided if it is required. The procedure followed in training—in fact, even wording of various commands—may vary from instructor to instructor. Equipment used will vary somewhat, also, but will usually include a training collar and leash such as those shown on page 109, a long line, a dumbbell, and a jumping stick.

The latter may be a short length of heavy doweling or a broom handle and both it and the dumbbell are usually painted white for increased visibility.

A bitch in season must never be taken to a training class, so before enrolling a female dog, you should determine whether she may be expected to come into season before classes are scheduled to end. If you think she will, it is better to wait and enroll her in a later course, rather than start the course and then miss classes for several weeks.

In addition to the time devoted to actual work in class, the dog must have regular, daily training sessions for practice at home. Before each class or home training session, the dog should be exercised so he will not be highly excited when the session starts, and he must be given an opportunity to relieve himself before the session begins. (Should he have an accident during the class, it is your responsibility to clean up after him.) The dog should be fed several hours before time for the class to begin or else after the class is over—never just before going to class.

If you decide to enter your dog in obedience competition, it is well to enter a small, informal show the first time. Dogs are usually called in the order in which their names appear in the catalog, so as soon as you arrive at the show, acquaint yourself with the schedule. If your dog is not the first to be judged, spend some time at ringside, observing the routine so you will know what to expect when your dog's turn comes.

In addition to collar, leash, and other equipment, you should take your dog's food and water pans and a supply of the food and water to which he is accustomed. You should also take his brushes and combs in order to give him a last-minute brushing before you enter the ring. It is important that the dog look his best even though he isn't to be judged on his appearance.

Before entering the ring, exercise your dog, give him a drink of water, and permit him to relieve himself. Once your dog enters the ring, give him your full attention and be sure to give voice commands distinctly so he will hear and understand, for there will be many distractions at ringside.

Top dogs in Utility Class. This illustrates variety of breeds that compete in obedience.

Genetics

Genetics, the science of heredity, deals with the processes by which physical and mental traits of parents are transmitted to offspring. For centuries, man has been trying to solve these puzzles, but only in the last two hundred years has significant progress been made.

During the eighteenth century, Kölreuter, a German scientist, made revolutionary discoveries concerning plant sexuality and hybridization but was unable to explain just how hereditary processes worked. In the middle of the nineteenth century, Gregor Johann Mendel, an Augustinian monk, experimented with the ordinary garden pea and made other discoveries of major significance. He found that an inherited characteristic was inherited as a complete unit, and that certain characteristics predominated over others. Next, he observed that the hereditary characteristics of each parent are contained in each offspring, even when they are not visible, and that "hidden" characteristics can be transferred without change in their nature to the grandchildren, or even later generations. Finally, he concluded that although heredity contains an element of uncertainty, some things are predictable on the basis of well-defined mathematical laws.

Unfortunately, Mendel's published paper went unheeded, and when he died in 1884 he was still virtually unknown to the scientific world. But other researchers were making discoveries, too. In 1900, three different scientists reported to learned societies that much of their research in hereditary principles had been proved years before by Gregor Mendel and that findings matched perfectly.

Thus, hereditary traits were proved to be transmitted through the chromosomes found in pairs in every living being, one of each pair contributed by the mother, the other by the father. Within each chromosome have been found hundreds of smaller structures, or genes, which are the actual determinants of hereditary characteristics. Some genes are dominant and will be seen in the offspring. Others are recessive and will not be outwardly apparent, yet can be passed on to the offspring to combine with a similar recessive gene of the other parent and thus be seen. Or they may be passed on to the offspring, not be outwardly apparent, but be passed on again to become apparent in a later generation.

Once the genetic theory of inheritance became widely known, scientists began drawing a well-defined line between inheritance and environment. More recent studies show some overlapping of these influences and indicate a combination of the two may be responsible for certain characteristics. For instance, studies have proved that extreme cold increases the amount of black pigment in the skin and hair of the "Himalayan" rabbit, although it has little or no effect on the white or colored rabbit. Current research also indicates that even though characteristics are determined by the genes, some environmental stress occurring at a particular period of pregnancy might cause physical change in the embryo.

Long before breeders had any knowledge of genetics, they practiced one of its most important principles—selective breeding. Experience quickly showed that "like begets like," and by breeding like with like and discarding unlike offspring, the various individual breeds were developed to the point where variations were relatively few. Selective breeding is based on the idea of maintaining the quality of a breed at the highest possible level, while improving whatever defects are prevalent. It requires that only the top dogs in a litter be kept for later breeding, and that inferior specimens be ruthlessly eliminated.

In planning any breeding program, the first requisite is a definite goal—that is, to have clearly in mind a definite picture of the type of dog you wish eventually to produce. To attempt to breed perfection is to approach the problem unrealistically. But if you don't breed for improvement, it is preferable that you not breed at all.

As a first step, you should select a bitch that exemplifies as many of the desired characteristics as possible and mate her with a dog that also has as many of the desired characteristics as possible. If you start with mediocre pets, you will produce mediocre pet puppies. If you decide to start with more than one bitch, all should closely approach the type you desire, since you will

Parents:
One pure dark eyes
and one pure light eyes

Dark eyes   Light eyes

Offspring:
Eyes dark (dominant) with light recessive

Parents:
With dark dominant and light recessive

¼ will be   ½ will be dark dominant   ¼ will be
pure dark   and light recessive   pure light

Offspring:

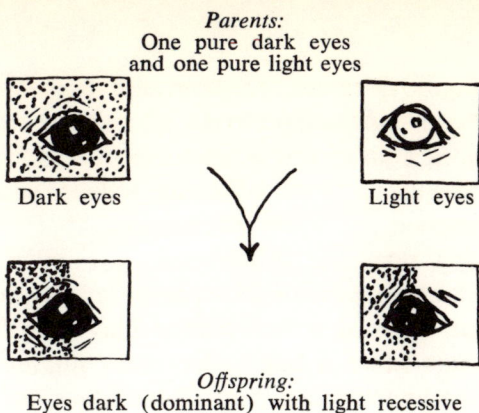

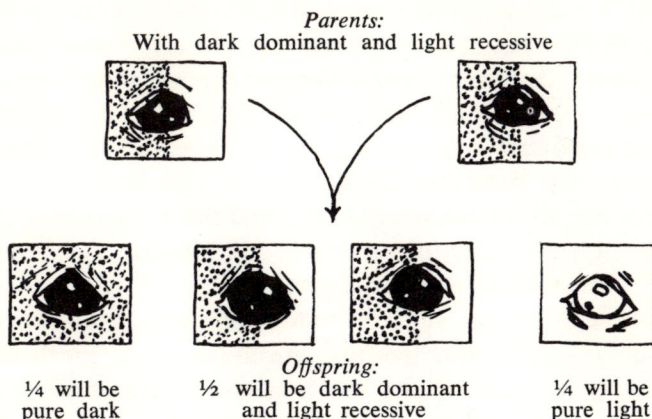

The above is a schematic representation of the Mendelian law as it applies to the inheritance of eye color. The law applies in the same way to the inheritance of other physical characteristics.

then stand a better chance of producing uniformly good puppies from all. Breeders often start with a single bitch and keep the best bitches in every succeeding generation.

Experienced breeders look for "prepotency" in breeding stock —that is, the ability of a dog or bitch to transmit traits to most or all of its offspring. While the term is usually used to describe the transmission of good qualities, a dog may also be prepotent in transmitting faults. To be prepotent in a practical sense, a dog must possess many characteristics controlled by dominant genes. If desired characteristics are recessive, they will be apparent in the offspring only if carried by both sire and dam. Prepotent dogs and bitches usually come from a line of prepotent ancestors, but the mere fact that a dog has exceptional ancestors will not necessarily mean that he himself will produce exceptional offspring.

A single dog may sire a tremendous number of puppies, whereas a bitch can produce only a comparatively few litters during her lifetime. Thus, a sire's influence may be very widespread as compared to that of a bitch. But in evaluating a particular litter, it must be remembered that the bitch has had as much influence as has had the dog.

Inbreeding, line-breeding, outcrossing, or a combination of the three are the methods commonly used in selective breeding.

Inbreeding is the mating together of closely related animals, such as father-daughter, mother-son, or brother-sister. Although some breeders insist such breeding will lead to the production of defective individuals, it is through rigid inbreeding that all breeds of dogs have been established. Controlled tests have shown that any harmful effects appear within the first five or ten generations, and that if rigid selection is exercised from the beginning, a vigorous inbred strain will be built up.

Line-breeding is also the mating together of individuals related by family lines. However, matings are made not so much on the basis of the dog's and bitch's relationship to each other, but, instead, on the basis of their relationship to a highly admired ancestor, with a view to perpetuating his qualities. Line-breeding constitutes a long-range program and cannot be accomplished in a single generation.

Outcrossing is the breeding together of two dogs that are unrelated in family lines. Actually, since breeds have been developed through the mating of close relatives, all dogs within any given breed are related to some extent. There are few breedings that are true outcrosses, but if there is no common ancestor within five generations, a mating is usually considered an outcross.

Experienced breeders sometimes outcross for one generation in order to eliminate a particular fault, then go back to inbreeding or line-breeding. Neither the good effects nor the bad effects of outcrossing can be truly evaluated in a single mating, for undesirable recessive traits may be introduced into a strain, yet not show up for several generations. Outcrossing is better left to experienced breeders, for continual outcrossing results in a wide variation in type and great uncertainty as to the results that may be expected.

Two serious defects that are believed heritable—subluxation and orchidism—should be zealously guarded against, and afflicted dogs and their offspring should be eliminated from breeding programs. Subluxation is a condition of the hip joint where the bone of the socket is eroded and the head of the thigh bone is also worn away, causing lameness which becomes progressively more serious until the dog is unable to walk. Orchidism is the failure of one or both testicles to develop and descend properly. When one testicle is involved, the term "monorchid" is used. When both are involved, "cryptorchid" is used. A cryptorchid is almost always sterile, whereas a monorchid is usually fertile. There is evidence that orchidism "runs in families" and that a monorchid transmits the tendency through bitch and male puppies alike.

Through the years, many misconceptions concerning heredity have been perpetuated. Perhaps the one most widely perpetuated is the idea evolved hundreds of years ago that somehow characteristics were passed on through the mixing of the blood of the parents. We still use terminology evolved from that theory when we speak of bloodlines, or describe individuals as full-blooded, despite the fact that the theory was disproved more than a century ago.

Also inaccurate and misleading is any statement that a definite fraction or proportion of an animal's inherited characteristics can be positively attributed to a particular ancestor. Individuals lacking knowledge of genetics sometimes declare that an individual receives half his inherited characteristics from each parent, a quarter from each grandparent, an eighth from each great-grandparent, etc. Thousands of volumes of scientific findings have been published, but no simple way has been found to determine positively which characteristics have been inherited from which ancestors, for the science of heredity is infinitely complex.

Any breeder interested in starting a serious breeding program should study several of the excellent books on canine genetics that are currently available.

Whelping box. Detail at right shows proper side-wall construction which helps keep small puppies confined and provides sheltered nook which to prevent crushing or smothering.

Breeding and Whelping

The breeding life of a bitch begins when she comes into season the first time at the age of about one to two years (depending on what breed she is). Thereafter, she will come in season at roughly six-month intervals, but this, too, is subject to variation. Her maximum fertility builds up from puberty to full maturity and then declines until a state of total sterility is reached in old age. Just when this occurs is hard to determine, for the fact that an older bitch shows signs of being in season doesn't necessarily mean she is still capable of reproducing.

The length of the season varies from eighteen to twenty-one days. The first indication is a pronounced swelling of the vulva with coincidental bleeding (called "showing color") for about the first seven to nine days. The discharge gradually turns to a creamy color, and it is during this phase (estrus), from about the tenth to the fifteenth days, that the bitch is ovulating and is receptive to the male. The ripe, unfertilized ova survive for about seventy-two hours. If fertilization doesn't occur, the ova die and are discharged the next time the bitch comes in season. If fertilization does take place, each ovum attaches itself to the walls of the uterus, a membrane forms to seal it off, and a foetus develops from it.

Following the estrus phase, the bitch is still in season until about the twenty-first day and will continue to be attractive to males, although she will usually fight them off as she did the first few days. Nevertheless, to avoid accidental mating, the bitch must be confined for the entire period. Virtual imprisonment is necessary, for male dogs display uncanny abilities in their efforts to reach a bitch in season.

The odor that attracts the males is present in the bitch's urine, so it is advisable to take her a good distance from the house before permitting her to relieve herself. To eliminate problems completely, your veterinarian can prescribe a preparation that will disguise the odor but will not interfere with breeding when the time is right. Many fanciers use such preparations when exhibit-

ing a bitch and find that nearby males show no interest whatso-
ever. But it is not advisable to permit a bitch to run loose when
she has been given a product of this type, for during estrus she
will seek the company of male dogs and an accidental mating
may occur.

A potential brood bitch, regardless of breed, should have good
bone, ample breadth and depth of ribbing, and adequate room
in the pelvic region. Unless a bitch is physically mature—well
beyond the puppy stage when she has her first season—breeding
should be delayed until her second or a later season. Furthermore,
even though it is possible for a bitch to conceive twice a year,
she should not be bred oftener than once a year. A bitch that is
bred too often will age prematurely and her puppies are likely
to lack vigor.

Two or three months before a bitch is to be mated, her physical condition should be considered carefully. If she is too thin,
provide a rich, balanced diet plus the regular exercise needed to
develop strong, supple muscles. Daily exercise on the lead is as
necessary for the too-thin bitch as for the too fat one, although
the latter will need more exercise and at a brisker pace, as well
as a reduction of food, if she is to be brought to optimum condition. A prospective brood bitch must have had permanent distemper shots as well as rabies vaccination. And a month before
her season is due, a veterinarian should examine a stool specimen
for worms. If there is evidence of infestation, the bitch should
be wormed.

A dog may be used at stud from the time he reaches physical
maturity, well on into old age. The first time your bitch is bred,
it is well to use a stud that has already proven his ability by
having sired other litters. The fact that a neighbor's dog is
readily available should not influence your choice, for to produce
the best puppies, you must select the stud most suitable from a
genetic standpoint.

If the stud you prefer is not going to be available at the time
your bitch is to be in season, you may wish to consult your
veterinarian concerning medications available for inhibiting the
onset of the season. With such preparations, the bitch's season
can be delayed indefinitely.

Usually the first service will be successful. However, if it isn't, in most cases an additional service is given free, provided the stud dog is still in the possession of the same owner. If the bitch misses, it may be because her cycle varies widely from normal. Through microscopic examination, a veterinarian can determine exactly when the bitch is entering the estrus phase and thus is likely to conceive.

The owner of the stud should give you a stud-service certificate, providing a four-generation pedigree for the sire and showing the date of mating. The litter registration application is completed only after the puppies are whelped, but it, too, must be signed by the owner of the stud as well as the owner of the bitch. Registration forms may be secured by writing The American Kennel Club.

In normal pregnancy there is usually visible enlargement of the abdomen by the end of the fifth week. By palpation (feeling with the fingers) a veterinarian may be able to distinguish developing puppies as early as three weeks after mating, but it is unwise for a novice to poke and prod, and try to detect the presence of unborn puppies.

The gestation period normally lasts nine weeks, although it may vary from sixty-one to sixty-five days. If it goes beyond sixty-five days from the date of mating, a veterinarian should be consulted.

During the first four or five weeks, the bitch should be permitted her normal amount of activity. As she becomes heavier, she should be walked on the lead, but strenuous running and jumping should be avoided. Her diet should be well balanced (see page 43), and if she should become constipated, small amounts of mineral oil may be added to her food.

A whelping box should be secured about two weeks before the puppies are due, and the bitch should start then to use it as her bed so she will be accustomed to it by the time puppies arrive. Preferably, the box should be square, with each side long enough so that the bitch can stretch out full length and have several inches to spare at either end. The bottom should be padded with an old cotton rug or other material that is easily laundered. Edges of the padding should be tacked to the floor of the box so the puppies will not get caught in it and smother. Once it is obvious labor is about to begin, the padding should be covered with several layers of spread-out newspapers. Then, as papers become soiled, the top layer can be pulled off, leaving the area clean.

Forty-eight to seventy-two hours before the litter is to be whelped, a definite change in the shape of the abdomen will be noted. Instead of looking barrel-shaped, the abdomen will sag pendulously. Breasts usually redden and become enlarged, and milk may be present a day or two before the puppies are whelped. As the time becomes imminent, the bitch will probably scratch and root at her bedding in an effort to make a nest, and will refuse food and ask to be let out every few minutes. But the surest sign is a drop in temperature of two or three degrees about twelve hours before labor begins.

The bitch's abdomen and flanks will contract sharply when labor actually starts, and for a few minutes she will attempt to expel a puppy, then rest for a while and try again. Someone should stay with the bitch the entire time whelping is taking place, and if she appears to be having unusual difficulties, a veterinarian should be called.

Puppies are usually born head first, though some may be born feet first and no difficulty encountered. Each puppy is enclosed in a separate membranous sac that the bitch will remove with her teeth. She will sever the umbilical cord, which will be attached to the soft, spongy afterbirth that is expelled right after the puppy emerges. Usually the bitch eats the afterbirth, so it is necessary to watch and make sure one is expelled for each puppy whelped. If afterbirth is retained, the bitch may develop peritonitis and die.

The dam will lick and nuzzle each newborn puppy until it is warm and dry and ready to nurse. If puppies arrive so close together that she can't take care of them, you can help her by rubbing the puppies dry with a soft cloth. If several have been whelped but the bitch continues to be in labor, all but one should be removed and placed in a small box lined with clean towels and warmed to about seventy degrees. The bitch will be calmer if one puppy is left with her at all times.

Whelping sometimes continues as long as twenty-four hours for a very large litter, but a litter of two or three puppies may be whelped in an hour. When the bitch settles down, curls around the puppies and nuzzles them to her, it usually indicates that all have been whelped.

The bitch should be taken away for a few minutes while you clean the box and arrange clean padding. If her coat is soiled, sponge it clean before she returns to the puppies. Once she is back in the box, offer her a bowl of warm beef broth and a pan of cool water, placing both where she will not have to get up in order to reach them. As soon as she indicates interest in food, give her a generous bowl of chopped meat to which codliver oil and dicalcium phosphate have been added (see page 43).

If inadequate amounts of calcium are provided during the period the puppies are nursing, eclampsia may develop. Symptoms are violent trembling, rapid rise in temperature, and rigidity of muscles. Veterinary assistance must be secured immediately, for death may result in a very short time. Treatment consists of massive doses of calcium gluconate administered intravenously, after which symptoms subside in a miraculously short time.

All puppies are born blind and their eyes open when they are ten to fourteen days old. At first the eyes have a bluish cast and appear weak, and the puppies must be protected from strong light until at least ten days after the eyes open.

To ensure proper emotional development, young dogs should be shielded from loud noises and rough handling. Being lifted by the front legs is painful and may result in permanent injury to the shoulders. So when lifting a puppy, always place one hand under the chest with the forefinger between the front legs, and place the other hand under his bottom.

Sometimes the puppies' nails are so long and sharp that they scratch the bitch's breasts. Since the nails are soft, they can be trimmed with ordinary scissors.

If of a breed that ordinarily has a docked tail, puppies should have their tails shortened when they are three days old. Dewclaws—thumblike appendages appearing on the inside of the legs of some breeds—are removed at the same time. While both are simple procedures, they shouldn't be attempted by amateurs.

In certain breeds it is customary to crop the ears, also. This should be done at about eight weeks of age. Cropping should never be attempted by anyone other than a veterinarian, for it requires use of anesthesia and knowledge of surgical techniques, as well as judgment as to the eventual size of the dog and proportion of ear to be removed so the head will be balanced when the dog is mature.

At about four weeks of age, formula should be provided. The amount fed each day should be increased over a period of two weeks, when the puppies can be weaned completely. The formula should be prepared as described on page 41, warmed to luke-warm, and poured into a shallow pan placed on the floor of the box. After his mouth has been dipped into the mixture a few times, a puppy will usually start to lap formula. All puppies should be allowed to eat from the same pan, but be sure the small ones get their share. If they are pushed aside, feed them separately. Permit the puppies to nurse part of the time, but gradually increase the number of meals of formula. By the time the puppies are five weeks old, the dam should be allowed with them only at night. When they are about six weeks old, they should be weaned completely and fed the puppy diet described on page 41.

Once they are weaned, puppies should be given temporary distemper injections every two weeks until they are old enough for permanent inoculations. At six weeks, stool specimens should be checked for worms, for almost without exception, puppies become infested. Specimens should be checked again at eight weeks, and as often thereafter as your veterinarian recommends.

Sometimes owners decide as a matter of convenience to have a bitch spayed or a male castrated. While this is recommended when a dog has a serious inheritable defect or when abnormalities of reproductive organs develop, in sound, normal purebred dogs, spaying a bitch or castrating a male may prove a definite disadvantage. The operations automatically bar dogs from competing in shows as well as precluding use for breeding. The operations are seldom dangerous, but they should not be performed without good reason.